SCOGIN ELAM AND BRAY

Critical Architecture / Architectural Criticism

RIZZOLI
NEW YORK

remembering Beppe Zambonini

SCOGIN ELAM AND BRAY

Critical Architecture / Architectural Criticism

edited by Mark Linder

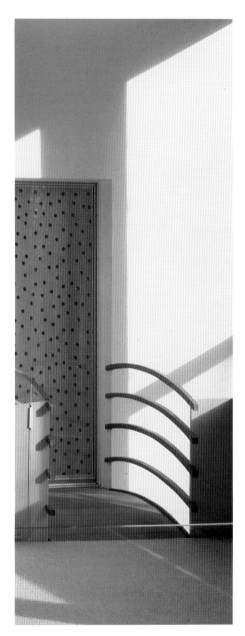

with essays by

Ann Bergren

Jeffrey Kipnis

Mark Linder

Alan Plattus

Anthony Vidler

Jennifer Wicke

RIZZOLI
NEW YORK

First published in the United States of America in 1992
by Rizzoli International Publications, Inc.
300 Park Avenue South, New York, N.Y. 10010

Library of Congress Cataloging-in-Publication Data
Scogin, Elam, and Bray:
critical architecture /architectural criticism /
edited by Mark Linder; with essays by Jeffrey Kipnis . . . (et al.).
p. cm.
Includes bibliographical references.

ISBN 0-8478-1534-X (hc) – ISBN 0-8478-1535-8 (pbk)
1. Scogin, Elam, and Bray.
2. Architecture, Modern – 20th century – United States.
I. Linder, Mark, 1960– . II. Kipnis, Jeffrey.
NA737.S365S37 1992   92-15638
720'.92'273 – dc20   CIP

Front cover: Chmar House
Back cover (hardcover only): Buckhead Library
Photographs by Timothy Hursley

Design and type composition by *Group* c

Printed and bound in Japan

Acknowledgments

This was a complex project and there are many people without whom it would never have been completed. It would not have even begun without the contributions of the many students at Georgia Tech who helped to organize, and implement the Critical Architecture/Architectural Criticism symposium: Stephen Amu, Ifhat Benayoun, David Green, Jean Heisel, Dawn Mixon, Caroline Reu, and Sam Van Nostrand. Most of all, I am grateful to Peter Green who spent many hours in the Scogin Elam and Bray archives, helping me to select numerous images and often saving me from my own bad judgement. Jeff Atwood of Scogin Elam and Bray helped me to find many drawings and always came through in a pinch. Jill Forte, the best administrative assistant ever, never balked at my piecemeal requests to transcribe the conference proceedings, and Jorge Delacova filled in admirably when Jill went on leave.

Brad Collins and Diane Kasprowicz were remarkable for their willingness to collaborate on the book's design and their persistence at turning my diagrams—however involuted—into a layout that works. Finally, I owe a special debt to Mack, Merrill, and Lloyd for their willingness to embark on this project and their consistent enthusiasm for its idea.

Grants and assistance from several sources made the symposium and book possible: the Architects' Society of Atlanta (special thanks to Jim Winer and Geddes Dowling), the Georgia Tech Foundation, the Architecture and Doctoral Programs at Georgia Tech, the Fulton County Arts Commission, and the High Museum of Atlanta. Corporate sponsors of the symposium include: Beers/BCB, Daugherty/Anderson Landscape Architects, Eberly and Associates, George Heery, Holder Construction, Humphries and Company, J. A. Jones Construction, Jones Nall Davis, Metric Constructors, Newcomb and Boyd Engineers, Palmer Brick and Tile, Pruitt Eberly Inc., John C. Portman and Associates, Reece Hoopes and Fincher, Land Planners-Landscape Architects, ROSSER FABRAP International, J. Ted Hall, and Gabriel Benzur Photography.

CONTENTS

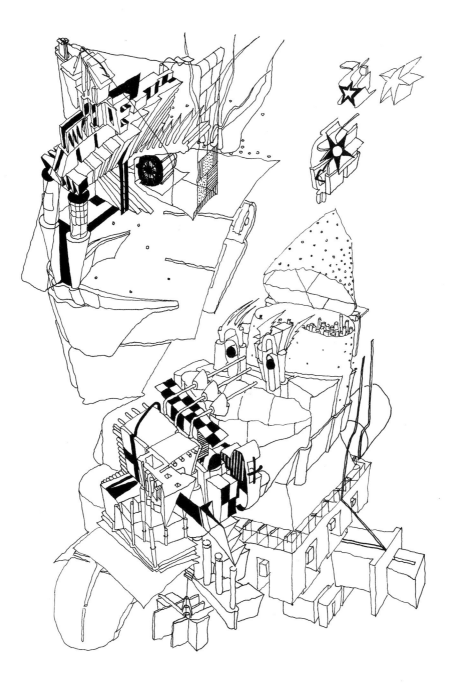

Preface

This book was conceived with a double purpose: it is a monograph on the architecture of Scogin Elam and Bray as well as an anthology of contemporary architectural criticism. The parity of this doubling constitutes a truly unusual union; because monographs conventionally focus single-mindedly on the presentation of architecture, their texts are subordinated (as commentary or description) to the images and drawings. In this book the writing and the architecture are conceived as equal partners that question the entirely common but nonetheless reductive tendency toward ranked oppositions, such as creativity over criticism, or theory over practice. The essays in this volume are not simple explanations of the architecture, just as the photographs and drawings are not readily revealed through written descriptions.

The very concept of a critical monograph assumes an active complicity between architecture and writing, responsibility and desire, criticism and design, taste and judgment, and so on—a complicity that is extremely complex and at times necessarily oblique. This book begins with the explicit recognition that architecture is implicated in the workings of a diverse and often confusing culture. The essays then bring that diversity to bear on the architecture of Scogin Elam and Bray (which itself exemplifies a kind of multiformity) with a desire to disseminate but not determine meaningful interpretations of the buildings, the practices that produce them, and the discourses that influence them.

It is an awareness of the intricacies of this transaction which convinces us of the value of this project, which began on May 12, 1990, as a symposium entitled "Critical Architecture/Architectural Criticism: The Work of Scogin Elam and Bray" at the High Museum of Art in Atlanta. By concentrating upon the architecture of a single firm, the conference established a forum in which to represent and discuss the difficulties and deficiencies inherent in the critical evaluation of architecture, to question accepted approaches to criticism, from the journalistic to the esoteric, and to offer a glimpse of the diversity of contemporary critical practices, including the professional practice of architecture. The proceedings of the symposium (six lectures, followed by a panel discussion), the questions raised there, and a complete presentation of the work of Scogin Elam and Bray make up the contents of this book.

These works of criticism and the project represented by the symposium and book would not be possible without a compelling and rich critical object. Because it is neither programmatically theoretical nor insistently pragmatic, the architecture of Scogin Elam and Bray offers an uncontestably intriguing object for critics and theorists. Their practice is markedly unconventional, but still participates in and reinterprets numerous architectural conventions, from modernism and economy to regionalism and the proprieties of professionalism. This ambitious work and the skillful subtlety of its forms provoke a reconsideration of what makes architecture critical, as well as a reformulation of prevalent approaches to architectural criticism.

My own essay clarifies and qualifies the conception of criticism that motivated and influenced the direction and objectives of this project. A preliminary version of that essay was given to the invited participants, along with a collection of slides and articles on Scogin Elam and Bray. Drawing upon these materials, each participant constructed a distinct approach to the practice of architectural criticism as well as to the practice of Scogin Elam and Bray. Jennifer Wicke offers a reading of the current critical scene that invokes the writings of David Harvey, Ernesto Laclau, and Chantal Mouffe, and criticizes the incessant allegorization of architecture inherent in so much contemporary theory. Her perspective, as a literary scholar, directs the discussion of criticism from the more specific, disciplinary concerns addressed in my essay toward more general conceptions of culture, space, and postmodernity. Anthony Vidler's essay develops an intricate historiographical discussion of monument and ornament (from Hegel to Vattimo) inspired by, yet external to, the specific practices of Scogin Elam and Bray. Alan Plattus, on the other hand, deploys a broadly conceived theoretical framework to explain how two of the firm's projects in Atlanta, the Chamber of Commerce building and the Herman Miller Showroom, manifest seemingly extreme concepts of difference in architecture. Jeffrey Kipnis discusses some of Mack Scogin and Merrill Elam's earliest projects—mostly competition entries—and argues against the idea of a critical architecture. His observations are presented here in the manner of a talk, a form of presentation which subtly complicates the interpretive framework instigated by the symposium and here revised by the format of the book. Ann Bergren instigates still more reconsideration of the format in her essay, which was conceived as an intricate *conférence* between incommensurate disciplines (classical mythology and architectural design), representational types (writing and photography), and cultural voices (the new South and Southern California). While the text printed here is basically a re-presentation of her lecture, the relationship of the words to the images has been fundamentally changed: when presented as a lecture, the images were more numerous and included fragments of the text and images of work by Scogin Elam and Bray as well as of seemingly extraneous material, some of which is retained here.

Thus, the book, through its design, encourages readers to participate in the speculative interplay of critical practices. While a relatively conventional reader may focus on the images and use the text to supplement an understanding of the architecture, a reader who is more interested in the problems of contemporary criticism will compare the various strategies, thus diverting primary attention from the architectural object. Still others will discern a conflict between the differing concerns of education and the profession (in both the critics and the architects), and perhaps some readers will consider the multiple voices as a microcosm of the current and competing

[1] See Umberto Eco, "Function and Sign: Semiotics of Architecture," *Via* 2 (1973): 132.

visions of contemporary architectural practice.

Each page is divided into three regions, each of which organizes a distinct type of information or material. In the center portion of each page and scrolling continuously through the book is the *text*; often it is displaced partially or entirely by *images* of the architecture of Scogin Elam and Bray. The relationship between the text and the images is not determinate: the images are not referenced specifically in the text and only rarely have captions. The images are organized to present each project on its own terms with varying degrees of correspondence to the discussion occurring in the text. Each project is introduced by a title—equivalent to those for each essay—and a small model photo. If one chooses to see the book as a collection of illustrations rather than a collection of illustrated essays, the text recedes into the background, yet the text has a background of its own. The bottom of each page contains the *context*; context entries are referenced in the text by bracketed letters, and page positions are established as purely visual relationships: that is, the context entries are located in line vertically with the bracketed letter. Context entries include excerpts from the symposium panel discussion [a.], extended notes to the text [b.], and selected short pieces of writing and illustrations other than those of the architecture of Scogin Elam and Bray, among them examples of the snapshots that the architects call their "favorite things" [c.]. Occasionally, if the amount of context material exceeds its normal boundaries, it encroaches upon the text region. Thus the text operates as the visual ground of the page and simultaneously assumes verbal priority. Finally, the *index* occupies the top of each page; it includes footnotes to the text and to the context text and/or images on the same page. It is ordered according to what Umberto Eco, after Charles Peirce, has called indexical signification, that is, its placement is determined by the relative position of the item it supplements.[1]

While the interplay of the four systems—text, image, context, and index—cannot definitively resolve the negotiations between criticism and architecture, and may even appear to exacerbate the problems that isolate those two practices, this book brings the rivals to the same table. The multiple order of the book's design reasserts, allegorically, the differences that frustrate architects and critics (not to mention historians, theorists, clients, and users) in their efforts to establish simple and direct means of collaboration. Perhaps only such seemingly devisive intricacies of structure can elicit intimacy among estranged parties.

Mark Linder, *Princeton, N.J.*

SCOGIN *I am not sure architectural criticism is existing any longer and I'm not sure there's any critical architecture. But it seems to me that we, my partners and our associates, could take a responsible role in helping to present the issue. I think that's the reason that we thought we would do this. To be honest, I am more uncomfortable right now than I think I have been in years for all sorts of reasons. To expose yourself in all the ways we allowed ourselves to be exposed. . . . I really can now understand why a lot of people don't do this. And I know damn well I won't do it again.*

KIPNIS *So you enjoyed it?*

SCOGIN *Well I did enjoy it.*

KIPNIS *The pleasure was too great; frightened by the pleasure you'll never do it again.*

SCOGIN *Well, I don't think that you're talking particularly about our work. But, I think our work was just the point of departure. I thought this was going to give us a certain level of comfort, which it didn't. It did make me think a lot about the history of our practice, the history of our experience in architecture, and sometimes that's pretty painful.*

Most context entries have been selected by the book's editor although some—such as this one—are extended footnotes written by the essay's author (who in this case is also the editor). In Ann Bergren's essay almost no context entries have been added by the editor.

a.　　　　b.　c.

Giving Critical Care

Mark Linder

This book and the symposium from which it has grown are efforts to devise and initiate a mode of intellectual production (or, to put it crudely, to fashion a criticism) that is neither complacent nor aestheticized and that evades the elitism, the scholasticism, and the star system of the present theory club, of which I must admit I am a junior member.

The dearth of contemporary discourse on architecture is rarely critical; architectural criticism will not be found in *Architecture*, *Progressive Architecture*, or *Architectural Record* because it is not promotion, information, or documentation. Although we may fashion criticism, criticism is not mere fashion. Neither is criticism gossip, commentary, or journalism. It is not harsh, negative, or unpleasant. Criticism *is* prospective and promising. Criticism is a project.

Whether architectural criticism builds upon the specifics of a site or uses a particular piece of architecture as its place of departure, actual architecture is the material of criticism, the fabric from which it is cut and toward which it weaves. Criticism spins yarns. Architectural criticism claims a specific complicity with the unraveling of architectural events. It *involves* writing: (as though) architecture matters, in the sense that we are often compelled to discuss "family matters" or "business matters." Criticism assumes that the matters of architectural fact are its family business. So, in every sense of the word, criticism gets involved.

I offer this description of criticism as a departure from or an alternative to (but certainly not a condemnation of) the continuing onslaught of what academics, practitioners, and commentators continue to call theory because, to be as direct as possible, theory in its current forms is feeble. Paradoxically, its weakness lies in its strength, which is to say, its clarity and its feigned disinterest, hence its inability to transform, reform, or inform. Architects in recent years have been struggling, with increasing signs of desperation, to deal with a proliferation of theoretical activity in architecture that has arisen to explain the new architecture and the conditions that have fostered it.

But the house of theory stands divided. On one side of the theory debate are those who desire that theory determine the form, and constitute the core, of architectural investigations. These (who might be called "traditional") theorists, in attempting to guide the actual process of design and to justify regulating the procedures of practice, tend to construct proposals aimed at situating and defining architecture; yet in spite of theoretical rigor their generalities fail to address the breadth of the architect's task. For the most part production of traditional theory has decreased in the last decade, as a second group of theorists has arisen that positions itself in the margins as an assemblage of commentators and adjudicators. These theorists speak broadly and persuasively about the conditions of intellectual culture at large and make compelling connections to other disciplines, yet the very extensiveness of their project rarely produces proposals for architectural action. Neither kind of theorist is serving the future of architecture well, not because either lacks keen insights or astute analyses but because each operates at the extremes of theory's potential. Adding to my list of negations, criticism is not theory. Theory and criticism do not serve the same purposes [a.].

Theory remains the term of choice within schools of architecture to describe speculative philosophical and literary research, although criticism makes the more immediately valuable and valid contribution to the education of architects and the production of new architecture. Criticism is an integral, prevalent, and effective part of design training. Students of architecture are likely to call their teachers "critics," and criticism, however impoverished or enriching, however authoritarian or dialogical its form, is enmeshed within the scene of instruction. Yet any critic must address the fact that architectural criticism remains weak in the professional culture of design practice. Many architects have turned not to criticism, as I am describing it, but to theoretical formulas for post-rationalization or to proscriptive criticism for policing (and ultimately judging) an unruly, threateningly talented, and irrepressibly ingenious mob.

As I understand these terms, one chooses criticism, rather than theory, out of dissatisfaction with the consequences and political alignments that the things called theory have provoked in architectural design. It means to want one's intellectual work to participate in the obsessions that compel designers, to be a conversant not a judge of results or an arbiter of design processes. It means to be preoccupied with any practice that is not only critical *of* but critical *to* the production of contemporary architecture and, more significantly, its inevitable reproduction (which need not be propagated as it is in the glossy magazines with their conspicuous consumption of images and their suspicious absence of actual criticism).

My dissatisfaction is further reinforced by the fact that the theoretical enterprise has yet to earn the respect of the common practitioner. Theory as we know it at best gives us directions; at worst, it directs us. Yet theory is perfectly avoidable; theory does not command attention. But this is not merely the fault of theory: architectural practice is becoming more and more of a service industry, in many ways indistinguishable from law, accounting, and financial advising. "Architecture" has become a "profession" in the service of capital, developing and preserving the exchange value of an extremely bulky and privately traded commodity. As architectural practice becomes ever more professionalized, architects will

KIPNIS *When I came into the city and I saw all of the new developments, some of it quite joyous and some of it quite disconcerting, I thought that Atlanta desperately needs someone to be making value judgments in an open forum, so as to create a kind of specific argument about the development of the city, particularly in the large-scale public sense. It's not that I apologize for myself or for the panel for not addressing the issue, but I do wonder if perhaps we should give some expressions to how that need in the city, and specifically in this city, might be situated in terms of some of our works. Do you think perhaps we should have addressed, more specifically, the kinds of judgments, critical judgments that would occur in a broader public forum?*

SCOGIN *Well, I can't imagine why you wouldn't want to.*

KIPNIS *You can't? Because in order to do that you enter the discussion of architecture as a participant in a local cultural and social fabric. You have to write as a metonymic voice; you have to write personal aspirations as a voice in the expectation that there will at least be some sort of general assent.*

SCOGIN *That's what we have to do to make architecture. We take on responsibility to make architecture. It seems to me that the writers and observers can take on responsibility to criticize and that the forums, like the High Museum and all of the other institutions in town, have the same responsibility and the same problem. I know how difficult it is. Making architecture is almost impossible. So I don't think you can sit back and say, well, that's just difficult.*

a.

1 Robert Somol,
"No Place Like Home:
Domesticating Assemblages,"
Assemblage 13 (1990):
69.

14

care less for architecture and design more architecture that does not let us care.

Too much theory positions itself in unnegotiable opposition to pervasive modes of practice. In the manner of all oppositions, it turns against the ordinary; it (vainly) proclaims revolution. Criticism on the other hand gets involved, that is, it tends toward involution. It does not turn against, it turns inward; it is introspective, involved, involuted, and inventive.

But perhaps my criticism of theory is not justified. I certainly do not want to be understood as being against theory; rather I am against some of its more particular and constrained versions. In fact, there is already a general drift by many theoreticians toward the view that theory has been (at least) misconceived and should be methodically interrogated or (at least) deconstructed, in the belief that we can find where the fault lies and expose its defects and deceptions. Deconstruction, or I should say Derrida, offers the most promising contemporary intellectual project. But Derrida's conception has become a contraption in the hands of those who exploit it; for them, it remains a theory about theory [b.]. This meta-approach is the line of the most vulgar deconstructors, operators of the mechanism of deconstruction who, in line with Enlightenment theory, operate the machine without necessarily understanding its reason [c.].

The machine operators (at least) bill deconstruction as a new paradigm of rationality, and in that sense it remains a defense of traditional theory, an enthused scandal to shield (preemptively) theory's vulnerability. Faced with real—and potentially lethal—terrorist actions from the margins (cultural, ethical, intellectual, political) that challenge the North-Atlantic intelligence empire, rationality is deployed to save itself, building glorious careers for *theorists* who outwit the *terrorists* at their own game [d.]. Intelligence thus gallantly preserves culture's foundations from destruction through deconstruction and under the ruse of critical thought canonizes artifacts of history—while revealing their weaknesses—by putting them on display in the theory museum [e.].

(It is as though the theorists believe that the terrorists will not blow up our buildings and bridges because we have declared them useless and surrounded them with velvet ropes and bright-eyed docents who envision themselves not as the parent-architects of the new order but as its impassioned homewreckers, compiling a massive scrap heap of used parts to be rummaged by the tinkers and bargain hunters

The storm is deconstruction, forgive me, deconstructivism. The architecture of the storm is hollow, forgive me, has been hollowed. This empty ranting has flattened its predecessors, forgive me, repeated their effacement. Is it an achievment to steamroll the already flat? Satisfaction reigns but I struggle to draw architecture from my flattened world. I build in the wake of abrasion, after the conflict of misfit thin-kings. I've read that power can be drawn from the debris, been convinced that from enclaves can blossom vast structures, and believe that it is in the domain of flatness that we now work. I look in the debris and find life. [excised, unused excerpt from elsewhere]

KIPNIS *There's also a personal point to make here. Deconstruction is constantly being referred to as a bankrupt practice because it constantly indulges itself in reframing undecidability; it is held as an accusation against the deconstructive process that it is unable to face a certain demand for social responsibility. In the recent Paul de Man controversy, for example, it was said that deconstruction fell back on well-known juridical techniques. I disagree. Deconstruction is writing about the desirability of different possibilities, and the desirability to augment decision frames and to keep their stabilities provisional. We have to be careful; I don't want anyone who's heard my work to leave saying that any work would graft equally well onto what I've said. That's relativism.*

VIDLER *I think underlying the question there might be a sense that, "Gosh, the architect is so clear, and these thinkers are so woolly."*

KIPNIS *Right.*

VIDLER *My sense is that it's the necessity of architecture to have a certain clarity, to resolve itself in a certain way, and it's a necessity of criticism to undo that, because it doesn't want to leave it as it is.*

Perhaps this distortion of Derrida is all too obvious, having been noticed even by pop musicians.

I'm in love with Jacques Derrida,
read a page,
I know I need to,
take apart my baby's heart.
I'm in love.

Scritti Pollitti

The compositions are curiously pure, clean and uncompromised. To paraphrase the opposed attitudes to art and politics that Benjamin develops, they tend to aestheticize garbage rather than trash art as high culture. [1]

d.   *b.*   c.   e.

2 Leon Battista Alberti,
   On the Art of Building in Ten Books,
   trans. Joseph Rykwert, Neil Leach,
   and Robert Tavernor
   (Cambridge, Mass.: MIT Press, 1988),
   34.

who fiddle idly in the safety of their basement workshops, ever yet under the delusion that they are on the cusp of a breakthrough.)

To object to such a domestication and display of the political means to believe that any theory that shoots itself in the foot in order to save its mind (or its self) espouses a reason that feigns madness, even entertains it, but remains recognizably rational (or merely shrewd). It makes up our minds but does not change our minds, and that is just what theory and criticism must do.

Why is criticism any better than theory? Criticism is nothing more than a promise (after all), but also nothing less. Because a promise is more than an agreement, or a contract, or a pact; it is a gift, just as talent, history, culture, philosophy, and architecture are gifts. Criticism eagerly accepts these gifts, but always with the suspicion that they are given not out of generosity but with the implicit design to encumber, to beholden, to require the proper respect not for the givers themselves but for the particular world that induces their giving.

Criticism never refuses these gifts. Nor does criticism return gifts or replace them in their boxes or remove them to the attic to be rediscovered upon criticism's own death. Criticism accepts gifts wholeheartedly, renaming them, revising them, and misusing them (often with great respect, while simultaneously displeasing the giver).

Of course, criticism must know a gift when it gets one, because criticism is the theory and the practice of gift-giving. More to the point, it makes a virtue of gift-getting. It shows us how better to receive. Criticism turns getting into giving. It turns promises into presence. To do criticism means to *make* a promise (present).

So, while theory usually tries to solve our problems and thereby save architecture, criticism is something like a salve, not only in the sense of a remedy for our ills, an ointment for our wounds, but in the sense of salvage. Criticism sifts through all of the trash in the world of contemporary architecture hoping to find something valuable. Criticism is not about saving capital, collecting scraps, or "aestheticizing garbage" but about dissolving artificial problems and recycling refuse. At its best, criticism turns garbage into a gift.

(Alberti gave us a gift in *Ten Books*. I accept it as such unconditionally, while I am wary of the power of its promise. He opens the second book by telling us to make models, the form of presentation which can best assist an understanding of our designs.

> Having constructed these models, it will be possible to examine clearly and consider thoroughly the relationship between between the site and the surrounding district, the shape of the area, the number and parts . . . the appearance of the walls, the strength of the covering, in short, the design and construction of all the elements. 2

In reading Alberti's *Ten Books*, I realize that what I call architectural criticism is strangely

3 Alberti,
Ten Books,
34.

4 Ibid.,
313.

5 Nelson Goodman,
Languages of Art:
An Approach to a Theory of Symbols
(Indianapolis: Hackett, 1976),
171.

16

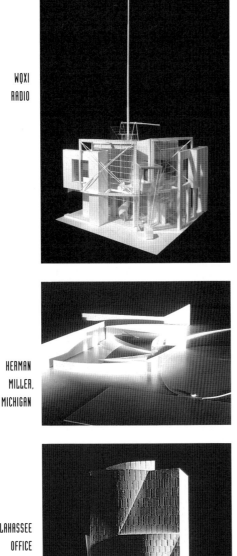

WQXI
RADIO

HERMAN
MILLER,
MICHIGAN

TALLAHASSEE
OFFICE
BUILDING

analogous to what he calls a model; I take from Alberti the belief that the best way to understand an architectural design is to model it, to construct a version that presents the issues at another scale and in another form. So, to do architectural criticism is to devise an architectural model, to offer a modeling of future architecture and a model-building [f.].)

In criticism, architecture turns into other architectural forms. All too often architectural theory is not architectural at all. My criticism of theory is that it too often builds illusory, nonarchitectural models, however beautiful or precious they may appear:

> The presentation of models that have been colored and lewdly dressed with the allurement of painting is the mark of . . . a conceited [architect], striving to attract and seduce the eyes of the beholder.[3]

> To avoid such pitfalls, therefore, I must urge you again and again, before embarking on the work, to weigh up the whole matter on your own and discuss it with experienced advisors. Using scale models, reexamine every part of your proposal two, three, four, seven—up to ten times, taking breaks in between.[4]

With the assistance of noncosmetic, critical models we architects can engage in what is literally a constructive conversation, one able to assist the reconstitution of architectural design as a healthy practice. Architectural criticism (as proposed here) is not about pronouncing the true, the good, and the beautiful; it is rather an attempt to continue, to reform, and to enrich architectural production. The practitioners of this criticism are often architects themselves, but more importantly their criticism takes the form of architecture. Just as to be *for* criticism is not to be *against* theory, criticism is not simply opposed to practice.

Criticism resides in an uneasy residual space that post-

I do not mean to offer an interpretation of Alberti's text but simply to exploit his gift and to admit the advantages, and current uncritical use, of the metaphor. Nelson Goodman provokes a similar interest:

> While scientists and philosophers have on the whole taken diagrams for granted, they have been forced to fret at some length about the nature and function of *models*. Few terms are used in popular and scientific discourse more promiscuously than 'model.' A model is something to be admired or emulated, a pattern, a case in point, a type, a prototype, a specimen, a mock-up, a mathematical description . . . and may bear to what it models almost any relation of symbolization.[5]

6 Manfredo Tafuri,
"The Historical Project"
in *The Sphere and the Labyrinth*,
trans. Pellegrino d'Acierno and Robert Connolly
(Cambridge, Mass.: MIT Press, 1987),
9.

7 Roland Barthes,
"What is Criticism?" in *Critical Essays*,
trans. Richard Howard
(Evanston: Northwestern
University Press, 1972),
257.

8 Tafuri,
"The Historical Project,"
12.
[all quotations this paragraph]

pones judgment by persistently questioning claims to authority; it opens up the domain of theory and the artifacts of practice; it requires a constant suspicion of the last word and avoids an authoritative voice. A critic is another sort of author who writes, designs, or builds not to establish a distinctive, definitive product—whether a style, persona, or position—but to extend the conversation, to compel the consideration of the possible. With or without a map, criticism negotiates the terrain of potentiality.

Yet this course involves many difficulties; Manfredo Tafuri announces the seemingly primitive capacities of any critical model.

> We could put it in another way and say that even the language of criticism, the language that should "move and break up stones," is itself a "stone." How are we to utilize it, then, to prevent it from becoming the instrument of a sacred rite? 6

Today we take anxious notice of the reasons why criticism does not present its contents as objective or its meanings as transparent. As Roland Barthes wrote almost thirty years ago in his famous essay "What is Criticism?" (1963):

> Criticism is more than discourse in the name of "true" principles. . . . All criticism must include in its discourse . . . an implicit reflection on itself; every criticism is a criticism of the work *and* a criticism of itself. In other words, it is essentially an activity. . . . Can an activity be "true?" 7

If we follow Barthes, we can immediately reject the notion that criticism is journalistic (or academic, to use Barthes' term), that it reports the facts in order to assert the truth. Tafuri has written similarly: "Criticism speaks only if the doubt with which it attacks the real turns back on itself as well." The critical project can be nothing less than a rebuilding of "the real," including a rebuilding of its own realm, its tactics, and its terms. "Criticism . . . will have to 'shift the stones' by shifting around its own stones." Like Wittgenstein's builders in *Philosophical Investigations* (who desire to construct a work of architecture with only four kinds of stones: beam, block, slab, and pillar), the critic is never quite certain what will arise from the work or if, in fact, the work will stand up (to subsequent criticism). Perhaps this is what Tafuri means when he writes that criticism "recognizes itself as an unsafe building." 8

Some of the seminal attempts to realize this kind of unsafe building lie in the diverse work of the artist Robert Smithson. His "nonsites" [g.], built of broken stones and contained only by geometric form-work, suggest not merely an unsafe building but the uncertainty of foundations, metaphysical or geological. It is his essays that offer some the earliest collusions of criticism and architecture. Smithson's wryly titled "Quasi-Infinities and the Waning of Space," published in the

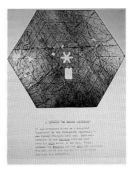

9 Robert Smithson,
"Quasi-Infinities and
the Waning of Space"
in *The Writings of Robert Smithson*
(New York: NYU Press, 1979),
32.

10 Tafuri,
"The Historical Project,"
7.

11 Walter Benjamin,
"The Work of Art in the Age
of Mechanical Reproduction"
in *Illuminations*,
trans. Harry. Zohn
(New York: Schocken Books, 1969),
233.

12 Smithson,
"A Tour of the Monuments
of Passaic, N.J."
in *Writings*,
52–53.

18

November 1966 issue of *Arts* magazine, initiates ingenious strategies for the construction of skepticism. The four-page essay consists of "four blocks of print" with "four ultramundane margins" that contain "indeterminate information as well as reproduced reproductions," [9] including numerous images of architecture [h.].

> With such "words," criticism—and not just architectural criticism—constantly constructs impenetrable monuments. The "stones" get piled up; their multiplicity is hidden by buildings that pretend (and pretend only) to give form to an "imaginary library." Or the opposite occurs: always leaving to the "stones" their indisputable density, caverns are excavated in their interstices. And so criticism finds itself obliged to make superfluous journeys. [10]

In 1967 Smithson published the deftly sarcastic essay "A Tour of the Monuments of Passaic, N.J.," which enacts Barthes' program via a "superfluous journey" through the ruined landscape of surburbia, insistently questioning the very tactics normally assumed as critical tools. Telling us about his arrival in Passaic by bus one Saturday, Smithson suspects his own observations, even as he dutifully records them on film. Smithson shows us that photography, which might easily be mistaken as a metaphor for objectivity, is more likely a metaphor for interpretation (and interpenetration). Unlike the piece of art criticism that he had read earlier that day in the *New York Times*, Smithson does not assume that his photographs portray the facts. The authority of photography is undermined as Smithson considers the implications of the images he records. Like Walter Benjamin, Smithson believes his camera does not distance him from his context but draws him "deeply into its web," [11] each picture further defining his relationship to the world of Passaic [i.].

> The bus passed over the first monument. . . . Noon-day sunshine cinema-ized the site, turning the bridge and the river into an over-exposed *picture*. Photographing it with my Instamatic 400 was like photographing a photograph. The sun became a monstrous light-bulb that projected a detached series of "stills" through my Instamatic into my eye. When I walked on the bridge, it was as though I was walking on an enormous photograph made of wood and steel, and underneath the river existed as an enormous movie film that showed nothing but a continuous blank. . . . I was completely controlled by the Instamatic (or what the rationalists call a camera). . . . I took snapshot after snapshot [12] [j.].

Another year later (1968), in "A Sedimentation of the Mind: Earth Projects," Smithson is more explicit (thus sabotaging himself in an act of criticism) about the fallacious claims of journalistic criticism.

> Journalism in the guise of art criticism fears the disruption of language, so it resorts to being "educational" and "historical." Art critics are generally poets who have betrayed their art, and instead have tried to turn art into a

j.   h.   i.

[13] Smithson, "A Sedimentation of the Mind: Earth Projects" in *Writings*, 87–88.

[14] Richard Rorty, "Professionalized Philosophy and Transcendentalist Culture" in *Consequences of Pragmatism* (Minneapolis: University of Minnesota Press, 1982), 66.

[15] Harold Bloom, *The Breaking of the Vessels* (Chicago: University of Chicago Press, 1982), 29.

[16] Harold Bloom and Lionel Trilling, *Romantic Poetry and Prose* (New York: Oxford University Press, 1973), 6.

matter of reasoned discourse, and, occasionally, when their "truth" breaks down, they resort to a poetic quote. Wittgenstein has shown us what can happen when language is "idealized," and that it is hopeless to try to fit language into some absolute logic, whereby everything objective can be tested. We have to fabricate our rules as we go along the avalanches of language and over the terraces of criticism[13] [k.].

Smithson's suggestion is that these landscapes, of which "Passaic, N.J." and "criticism" are but two examples, remain largely uncharted and constantly shifting. His sense of the limits of linguistic precision and his joy at exploding the containers of meaning are at the root of the form of criticism that I am advocating. Admittedly, this is a highly romantic form of thinking. Barthes and Smithson, in the process of confirming the freedom of language, are confronting the aged humanist belief that it is our privilege, as rational beings, to ascertain and assert the form and principles of the ideal [l.].

The romantic era granted us the sources of the criticism that I am trying to articulate or at least to evoke [m.]. Much like what is called "cultural criticism," it often takes the essay form. In the words of Richard Rorty, criticism "is neither the evaluation of the relative merits of literary productions, nor intellectual history, nor moral philosophy, nor epistemology, nor social prophecy, but all these things mingled together into a new genre."[14] This description applies directly to texts such as the now infamous chapter of Victor Hugo's novel *Notre Dame* titled "This Will Kill That." Part narrative, part technological history, part social and urban theory, the chapter exemplifies Rorty's criticism and is critical *to* any romantic modeling of modern architecture. In that essay Hugo announces that the building has been subsumed by the book, implicating the printed word in the assassination of architecture and usurping architecture's claim to embody and articulate meaning in a way that gives life to culture. The invention of the printing press has caused the demise of architecture's status as privileged vessel of meaning. The printed word and the proliferation of the book have forced architecture into literary obsolescence.

> Printing! And make no mistake about it! Architecture is dead, irrevocably dead, killed by the printed book. . . . The great poem, the great

VIDLER *The way in which Mark set this conference up, by giving us an object of study (slides and essays) for a long time before we came here (whether or not the papers themselves went directly to the heart of particular buildings) certainly, in my case, formed the way in which I thought about the paper I wrote and precisely raised the issues about which I was interested. If that object of study had been a map of Atlanta as opposed to photos of buildings and projects by Scogin Elam and Bray, I'm sure that in the symposium we would all address issues of urban judgments and the problems of urban fabric in relationship to the architectural object. What I find very exhilarating about today is that it wasn't just a group of critics talking about criticism, nor was it just a group of journalists commenting on a body of work. It was a group of people searching for ways to address work that didn't repeat the work itself on its own terms. Walter Benjamin made a distinction between what he called criticism and commentary. Commentary is something that journalists do a lot of. They describe the work in the work's own terms or the event in the event's own terms. They don't touch it. Mark mentioned the romantic foundations of critical thought. It is very clear that Benjamin was looking at the German romantics as figures who could construct discourse, if you like, outside the object that they were discussing but so deeply linked to it that once they had brought the two things together, they were changed. If we sometimes seem to be circling around like birds of prey, looking for things to pick up on, it is precisely because none of us feel that criticism should leave the work untouched, even if some of us didn't get further than making matrixes for beginning to do that.*

Most important to this understanding of the language of criticism is Smithson's assertion that a critic ought to be a poet or, as the arch-romantic Harold Bloom puts it, "The language of poetry and the language of criticism cannot differ in more than degree."[15] Bloom's claim is that to be a poet today (in the English language at least) means still to be a romantic, as is powerfully evident in the mythology of romantic love. According to Bloom, "Romanticism offers a vision of desire as being its own value, with necessarily a counterversion of hell as failed or frustrated desire."[16]

```
BEAMBLOCKSLABPILLAR
PILLARBEAMBLOCKSLAB
SLABPILLARBEAMBLOCK
BLOCKSLABPILLARBEAM
```

m.   l.   k.

17 Victor Hugo,
The Hunchback of Notre Dame,
trans. Walter Cobb
(New York: Penguin, 1965 [1831]),
186.

18 Hugo,
The Hunchback of Notre Dame,
187–88.

19 Barthes,
Image—Music—Text,
trans. Stephen Heath
(New York: Hill and Wang, 1977),
25–26.

structure, the great masterwork of humanity will never again be built; it will be printed. And, besides, if, by chance, architecture should be revived, it will never again be mistress. It will submit to the laws of literature which once received its laws from architecture. [17]

One building that vividly acts out this transformation, as Neil Levine has suggested, is the Bibliothèque St. Geneviève, which on one level serves as a gigantic bookcase and on another depends explicitly upon language to denote its significance, its outside panels reading like a huge card catalogue [n.]. But criticism, unlike the library (or for that matter, the nineteenth-century museum) does not categorize or classify, and therefore equalize, its contents.

Another case of this transference of literary value is the development of the commercial newspaper. Jennifer Wicke writes in *Advertising Fictions* that the newspaper's demand for commercial advertisements provided yet another site in which to assert literary meaning and in turn demanded new visual and linguistic strategies that drew upon photography, the novel, and popular art. More provocatively, the arbitrary juxtapositions engendered by the placement of ads, articles, and images in the newspaper suggests a flatly complicit architecture of the page. This development has compelled the invention not only of new techniques of printing but of new methods of reading that Hugo could never have envisioned [o.] [p.].

Quite simply, the proliferation of reproductive techniques from the printing press to the camera and, more recently, the dazzling capabilities of computer-enhanced video extends Hugo's argument and propels us into a situation in which literary values (so the story goes) once carried by architecture are compressed effectively onto the two-dimensional page or screen.

Hugo assumes, though, that the advent of reproduction implies the demise of architecture; he does not consider that it remains entirely possible to have a critical coupling of this and that [q.]. With this suggestion of symbiosis, I would like to turn Hugo on his head. In fact, a careful reading of *Notre Dame* suggests not that the book has killed the building but that the book is itself a form of building. Hugo writes at the end of the chapter:

> If we try to form a collective picture of the combined results of printing down to modern times, does not this total picture seem to us like an immense structure, having the whole world for its foundation, a building upon which humanity has worked without cease and whose monstrous head is lost in the impenetrable mist of the future? . . . The building has a thousand stories. . . . However the prodigious building remains forever incomplete. The press, that giant engine, incessantly gorging all the intellectual sap of society, incessantly vomits new material for its work. The entire human race is its scaffolding. Every mind is its mason. Even the humblest may block a hole or lay a stone. . . . It is the second Tower of Babel of the human race. [18]

Roland Barthes also turns Hugo around, claiming that the newspaper has compelled "an important historical reversal, the image no longer *illustrates* the words; it is now the words which, structurally, are parasitic on the image. . . . Formerly, the image illustrated the text (made it clearer); today, the text loads the image, burdening it with a culture, a moral, an imagination. Formerly, there was a reduction from text to image; today, there is amplification from the one to the other." [19]

q.   n.   o.   p.

20 Ralph Waldo Emerson,
"The Poet" in *The Selected
Writings of Ralph Waldo Emerson*,
ed. Brooks Atkinson
(New York: Modern Library, 1940),
323.

21 Jacques Derrida,
The Truth in Painting,
trans. Geoff Bennington
(Chicago: University of
Chicago Press, 1987),
50.

22 Leo Steinberg,
"Other Criteria"
in *Other Criteria*
(New York:
Oxford University
Press, 1972),
82–91.

23 Tafuri,
"The Historical
Project,"
15.

24 Douglas Crimp,
"On the Museum's Ruins,"
in *The Anti-Aesthetic: Essays
on Postmodern Culture*,
ed. Hal Foster (Port Townsend,
Wash.: Bay Press, 1983),
47.

25 Jean-François Lyotard,
"Passages from *Le Mur du Pacifique*,"
trans. Pierre Brochet, Nick Royle,
and Kathleen Woodward,
The Lyotard Reader, ed. Andrew Benjamin
(Cambridge: Basil Blackwell, 1989),
66–67.

Hugo's invocation of the architectural metaphor aligns him with numerous other thinkers whose domain also is that of flatness (philosophers and painters, for example) and who claim that architecture has not been overwhelmed or exceeded by language but rather that language admits its codependence; all forms of writing reveal the necessity of architecture. Just ten years after Hugo's novel Emerson remarks in his essay "The Poet" that "argument is secondary, the *finish* of the verses is primary. . . . A poem . . . has an architecture of its own."[20] In a much more recent work, *The Truth in Painting*, Derrida pushes this understanding to the point of material comparison, saying that we can wander around a book much as we can a work of architecture: "A book . . . is a sort of architecture [and] the force of reading may depend, as with a piece of architecture, on the point of view. . . . There are only ever points of view, but the solidity, the existence, the structure of the edifice do not depend on them."[21]

Another analogy can be made regarding the "combines" of Robert Rauschenberg. His dissatisfaction with intellectualized painting, with the understanding of painting as a sort of window in which one discerns a pictorial order and a formal logic, led him to use what Leo Steinberg first called the "flatbed picture plane,"[22] in which the canvas operates in a manner analogous to the printed page. Rauschenberg rejected the canvas as the site of naturalized pictorial images and instead resituated it horizontally, in a prone position to receive and combine any number and kind of cultural images, artifacts, or materials [r.] [s.]. The horizontal flatbed evokes the phenomenological relationships not only of the printed page but of the architectural ground plan. Steinberg also claims that Rauschenberg participates in a "radical shift in the subject matter of art, the shift from nature to culture," but he has also shifted from techniques of production to those of reproduction in a manner not incongruous with Tafuri's proposal that "the critical act will consist of a recomposition of the fragments once they are historicized: in their 'remontage'"[23] [t.].

In these various ways Rauschenberg (not Goldberger), the commercial newspaper advertisement (not journalism), and the finish of poetry (not the rigor of measure) provide the precedents for an architectural criticism. As Douglas Crimp writes, Rauschenberg employed "a radically different pictorial logic,"[24] an understanding which I would like to extend to architectural criticism. Through the manner in which it adapts various modes of reproduction, through its explicit recogni-

The white authorities pass themselves off as those who give. This trade, at the base of which is the enjoyment of women . . . allows the white authorities to take the place of the white female center; but only the latter has potency—meaning, the potential to receive. Usurpation of potencies, imposture of functions. Every Caesar is this same impostor . . . who negotiates for what he believes are women, but actually he just negotiates for one of the results (himself being another one) of the auctioning of this white, empty expanse of space.[25]

t.   r. s.

26 Alan Colquhoun,
"From *Bricolage* to Myth,
or How to Put Humpty-Dumpty Together Again"
in *Essays in Architectural Criticism*
(Cambridge, Mass.: MIT Press, 1981),
169.

27 Lyotard,
The Lyotard Reader,
59.

28 Richard Rorty,
"Philosophy as a Kind of Writing:
An Essay on Derrida"
in *Consequences,*
108.

22

tion of the architecture of language, and through its self-described characterization as an activity, architectural criticism enacts what I would call a *radically different pictorial logic of the essay* [u.] [v.].

Architectural criticism, then, is a manner of writing in forms that are themselves architectural and that strive to make links across disciplines (or at their most audacious, to dedisciplinize) in order to compare and contrast normative but incomparable procedures such as design, theory, and history. Criticism operates in-between the territories staked out by systematic disciplines in a space that Alan Colquhoun calls "a no-man's-land between enthusiasm and doubt, between poetic sympathy and analysis. Its purpose is not, except in rare cases, either to eulogize or condemn, and it can never grasp the essence of the work it discusses."[26] [w.]

Perhaps it is
not too licentious to interpret
Colquhoun's gender reference
as a recognition that the critic
works in the outskirts of the
city of theory:

Invasions from the outskirts
create a metropolis, according
to the permeability of its
frontiers, the suppleness of
its skin. And inversely, the
naivete of whiteness, so
central, blackens everything
that desires its whiteness. [27]

The city of theory
is the "City of Real Men," as
Rorty dubs the city where systematic thinkers undertake the
"mighty time-binding work of
building the edifice of human
knowledge."[28]

Six Principles of
Architectural Criticism:

Theoretically thinness/
textually thickness 1
Unstable structure 2
Assembled incommensurables 3
Visual/verbal ambiguity 4
Specific materials 5
Seamless reproduction 6

w.   u.   v.

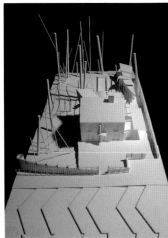

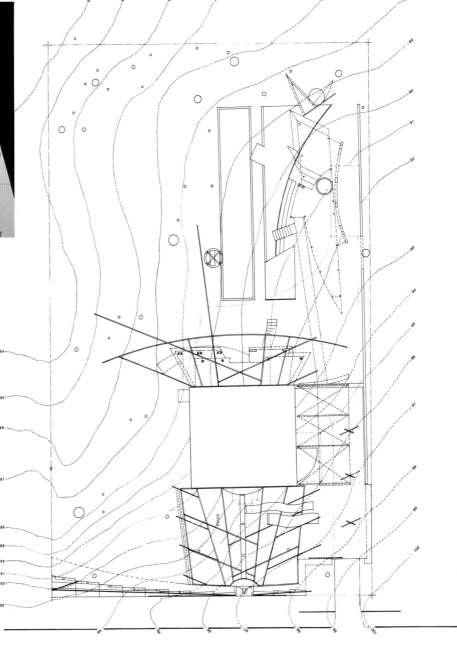

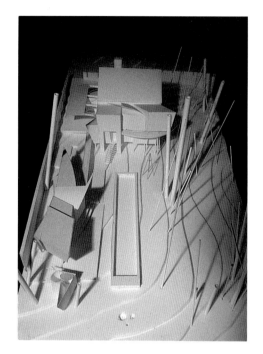

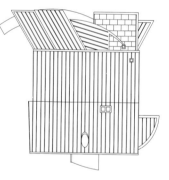

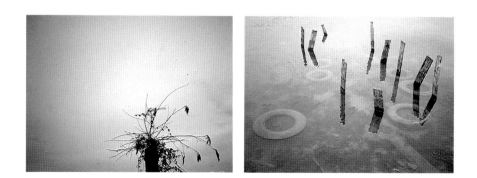

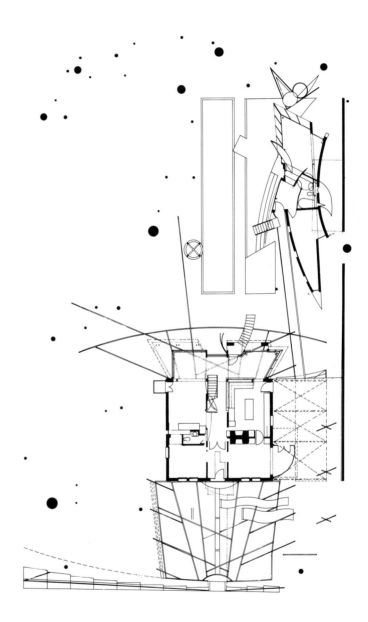

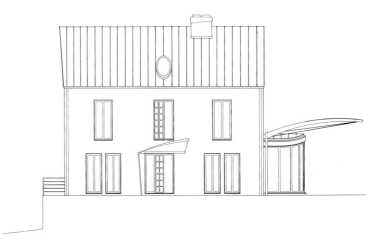

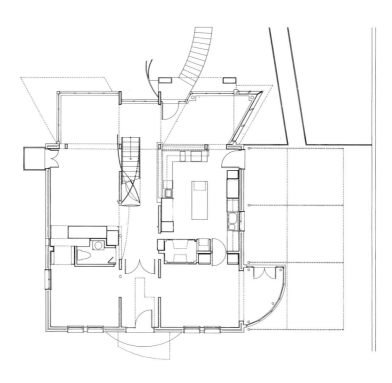

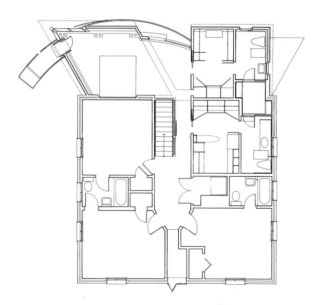

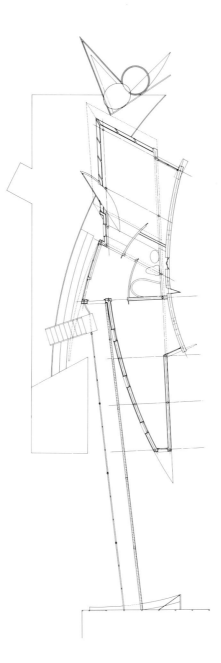

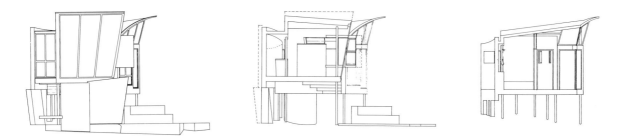

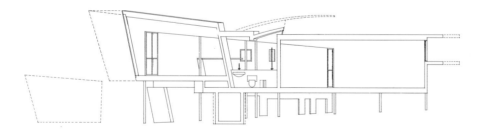

Picking up the Pieces

Jeffrey Kipnis

I Touring the work of Scogin Elam and Bray, I must admit to a feeling of some relief. Soon after being invited to participate in the "Critical Architecture/Architectural Criticism" conference, I spoke briefly to Mack Scogin and Merrill Elam, who were somewhat concerned about critics discussing their work without having actually visited it. For reasons that I will briefly elaborate, I am not in simple agreement with the view that the self-evident final arbiter for critical evaluation of a building rests in the direct experience of it. Yet I am sensitive to this issue and so decided to confine these remarks to certain material marginal to the built work of Scogin Elam and Bray such as competition projects by Elam, Scogin and others dating back six to eight years. Thus I avoid the problem of not having visited the buildings. Moreover, I believe that in so doing I might be better able to speak to the critical component of the work, i.e., that part of the work that submits to consideration as critical architecture.

The relief I felt derived from the fact that my encounter with the buildings—the Buckhead Library, the Herman Miller Showroom, the Candler School of Theology, the High Museum at Georgia Pacific Center, the Atlanta Chamber of Commerce, and the Chmar House—presented themes very different from those of the projects I discuss, even those of these very buildings when they were projects [a.]. In a certain sense, the least important issue for me at that on-site moment of encounter was how well or poorly the building embodies the ideas and thematic proposals of the project. The insistent experiential presence of these buildings, their materiality, symbolism, aesthetics, haptic and perceptual effects, relationships to sites, etc. simply dominated any other critical or thematic engagements of the work. It is precisely this dominance of presence that accounts for the virtually uncontested privilege afforded direct experience in architectural criticism. How often have we heard some variation of the phrase, "You cannot really understand the building until you visit it." Rightly so, no doubt, for if producing experience is what a building mainly does, should not the experience produced always be the ultimate critical test?

Yet some problems arise in this privileging of experience as a critical tool. The first and most familiar derives from the fact that experience itself is neither naive nor natural. Rather, it is artifactual, transformable, and constructed. The most conservative consequence of this artifactuality yields the all-too-familiar theme of connoisseurship, the critic as experienced or informed experiencer. The more interesting and radical consequence of the artifactuality of experience—that experience is always a contextual construct—underwrites the Marxist lineage of criticism. From this point of view naive experiential criticism and connoisseurship both serve the same agenda: maintaining the prevailing order. The problem for both

The day before the conference, the participants were driven by van to visit all but two of the Scogin Elam and Bray projects in Atlanta, to fulfill the wishes of the architects that everyone experience the built work and understand its context in the city of Atlanta.

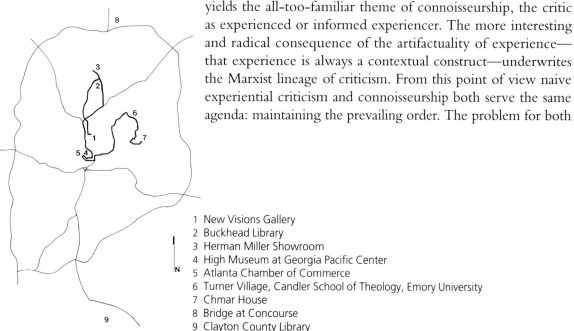

1 New Visions Gallery
2 Buckhead Library
3 Herman Miller Showroom
4 High Museum at Georgia Pacific Center
5 Atlanta Chamber of Commerce
6 Turner Village, Candler School of Theology, Emory University
7 Chmar House
8 Bridge at Concourse
9 Clayton County Library

1 Heinrich Wöfflin,
Principles of Art History
(New York: Dover, 1950 [1915]),
230.

2 Jeffrey Kipnis,
"Drawing a Conclusion"
Perspecta 22 (1986):
97, 99.

artist and critic is to reconstruct the context, to transform both the context and the experiencer by transforming experience.

In both of these sophistications—informed experience and transformed experience—direct experience and therefore presence retains its status. Post-structuralist criticism, on the other hand, draws a different conclusion [b.]. If the terms and conditions of the direct experience of a building are a contextual construct, they nevertheless constitute but one context of a building, however important that particular context may be.

Consider, for example, the art historian Heinrich Wölfflin's famous formula in *Principles of Art History*, "The effect of picture on picture as a factor in style is much more important than what comes directly from the imitation of nature."[1] This formula, of course, forms one of the founding tenets of structural formalism in art history. But for our purposes, we should note the dual effect of the statement. First it recognizes at least two contexts in which a painting participates, the disciplinary (painting/painting) and the representational (painting/nature). Second, the statement makes a value argument about the priority of one context of over another. One interpretation of Wölfflin's proposition in architectural terms is that the effect of building on building is more important to design criticism than the effect of building on sensory experience.

In any case, a post-structuralist critical position notes that architectural design participates in and inflects many contexts at one and the same time, not all centered on the experiential qualities of a building and its relationship to the site. Social and political theory, philosophical discourse, style, and fashion are examples of such contexts. This position claims that context is, strictly speaking, undecidable; no determination of a final or ultimate context is possible. Therefore, privileging one context over another, accomplished only by violent suppression, cannot be grounded in ontological or epistemological terms; such a judgment is always a political act.

The post-structuralist critic is more interested in the multiplicity of contextual participation than in the debate for or against the preeminence of one or another context. Assessing the nature and consequence of architecture's participation in these varying domains is not necessarily best accomplished by direct experience. Surely the plan of Palladio's Villa Rotunda is not best understood by the experience it creates.

Much of the attention of architectural theory over the last twenty years has been devoted to examining the mechanisms by which architectural design insinuates itself into different contexts. Likewise, much of the debate in architectural criticism has been about whether architecture's ability to transform contexts should be placed in the service of: 1) making a specific context better defined (contextualism, post-modernism); 2) breaking and redefining a specific context (the various -tech architectures, deconstructivism, the new avant-garde); or 3) rendering the contex-

In order to finish our "drawing" and bring it to a "conclusion," we should first look at the material of architecture, the "concrete form," if for no other reason than to confirm the visibility of its physical presence. After all, when we have the object in front of our eyes—the "door," the "loggia," the "villa," the "modern skyscraper"—we do not rely on any figurative metaphor to inform us of what we are seeing. Or is the "thing" we are "seeing" already a metaphor? Is the "doorness" of a physical door not actually a response, a *reading* of that concrete form's relation to other forms? . . . Our preliminary drawing, then, is the nonconclusion that a "theoretical article" is as much a "piece of architecture itself" as an architectural object is an article of discourse, of theory.[2]

b.

tual participation of the building more fluid and less decidable.

In any case, my point is simply this. To the critic or theorist interested in these latter issues—in context breaking and fluidity—the measure of architecture may well be more available at the project level, free of the overwhelming influence of a building's presence.

Obviously, the material of the project is very different from that of the building; it includes texts, analyses, definitions of the contexts, and so on. Though architecture adores presence, it feels compelled to authenticate its work in terms of transformative potential. That is why at the project stage every move—even those devoted to producing experience—is shaped by the architect's transformative vocation. All the more so if the emphasis is on context breaking or contextual fluidity. Later on, when we turn our attention to Elam's parking lot project, we will revisit this issue.

There are other reasons for my particular interest in projects. If you think about it for a moment, architecture effects an uncanny structural reversal by applying the hypnotic talents of presence. The common logic of the copy/original or representation/real holds that the latter is diminished by the former. The copy always comes after, points to, differs from, defers to, and violates the original, thereby reducing and weakening it. The copy mobilizes the original, allowing it to disseminate as if in an economy, but always at the risk of reducing the original to a commodity. Even though deconstruction has thoroughly and convincingly undermined this familiar morality play, one cannot deny that the copy/original value structure retains its full force even today. Allow me to close this section with a few questions: Strictly speaking, is not the building a copy of the project? Does not the building come after, point to, differ from, and, in a certain sense, violate the project, yoking it to the experiential presence? In architecture, therefore, is not the project the original, deserving the attention and status accorded other originals? And finally, if the building is a copy, is presence not the particular violence that such a copy visits upon its origins?

II Another issue became apparent to me upon visiting the buildings: the emergence in the built work (and specific to it) of Scogin Elam and Bray of what has been variously called personality, style, or signature but that I prefer to term *idiom*. Idiom is that aspect of work which is objective (i.e., not a matter of expression) yet singular. A consequence, perhaps, of authoring yet not authored in the classical intentional or gestural sense, idiom is the "life-of-its-own" of a body of work that always exceeds any and every analytic—intentional, historical, rhetorical, theoretical, philosophical, biographical, or psychological, yet poorly served when gathered under the like of such romantic/individualist euphemisms as the ineffable or the *je ne sais quoi*. As idiom develops it is both collaborator with and antagonist to authorship.

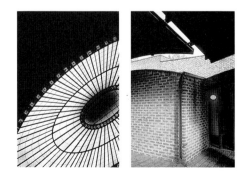

That idiom cannot be analyzed does not mean that it cannot be articulated. After all, one has no difficulty in articulating the exorbitance of water to a scientific analytic—that is, to comprehension in terms of hydrogen, oxygen, 105-degree polar covalent bonds, Van der Wals forces, and so forth. That every analytic that attempts to specify the "waterness" of water and to take control of the scientific, semiotic, and/or erotic proliferations of the complex of water—as stuff, as written and spoken word, as figure, and so forth—will fall short does not mean that the falling-short-as-such cannot give itself over to thought.

III   As I moved from building to building, I realized that, aside from the traditional issues that privilege the immediate experience of built work, also at stake was the emergence of an idiom. Connected largely to material technique, this developing idiom is beginning to operate in the work independent of such critical determinants as authorship, site, and program. The Scogin Elam and Bray idiom deserves discussion. Though I will not undertake that treatment here, I believe that these remarks will in some small way set a stage for that more interesting discussion.

A host of connections and coincidences entangle the margins of my architectural life with that of Merrill Elam and Mack Scogin. For example, it was during the "Tower to Southern Memories" competition held at the Atlanta Piedmont Arts Festival in 1982 and won by Elam that I first met Peter Eisenman and began a relationship that continues to condition my involvement with architecture. Of all of the many coincidences, however, the strangest for me is that I gave my first public lecture exactly seven years prior to presenting these remarks.

On the second Saturday in May 1983 I gave a talk called "Correct Close Reading: A Priority of Criticism" to the Architectural Society of Atlanta at the invitation of Merrill Elam and Mack Scogin. In that talk I expressed my personal and intellectual discomfort with what I considered to be art criticism's obsession with fixing the meaning of an art object, that is, with correct close reading. I tried to account for this obsession, which I viewed as evidencing a systematic compulsion to take control over a certain threat, a danger posed by objects in general that became intolerable at the level of the art object. Finally, I wanted to consider on what terms and by what mechanisms art objects both participated in and resist that critical obsession. After all, one cannot ignore that art objects seem not only to fuel critical fervor but always to gratify it—almost, while in the end always deflecting and rendering futile each new critical project no matter how subtle or probing.

Indeed, my interests have not changed very much in seven years. Though I now focus all of my attention on architecture, I continue to be moved by similar concerns. Like art, architecture is a discipline in which the critical obsession for control—for fixing the context, in terms of my earlier discussion—is distinctly marked. It is also a discipline in which the participation/deferral mechanisms of its performances are strongly indicated.

3 James Mount,
"Vers une Architecture Americaine,"
The American Dream, ed. Claire Downey
(Atlanta: Georgia Institute of Technology, 1983),
55.

Thus, my hopes here today are twofold: to outline a critique of a certain formulation of critical architecture and to propose that the measure of Scogin, Elam and Bray's architecture is to be found in the degree to which it subverts a rigorous notion of criticality. Some care is necessary here, however, for I do not mean to oppose the critical to the intuitive, the natural, the traditional, the normal, the self-evident, or any other force or condition. I do not mean to oppose the critical at all, for opposition is the critical gesture. Rather, I hope to elude it, to participate in it, to subvert it by offering little resistance to it, and, finally, to claim that architecture is most virtuous at the moment of its unresisting ellipses of the critical.

IV   One oddity of architectural discourse is how often the theme of critical architecture appears yet how vague the notion is. Unlike other disciplines such as philosophy, literary studies, or law, where the term *critical* is reasonably well specified, in architectural discourse the term is applied haphazardly, meaning anything from simply unusual to ideological or intellectual. In the literature such disparate architectures as those of Leon Krier, Aldo Rossi, Peter Eisenman, Tadao Ando, Frank Gehry, Daniel Libeskind, Harry Wolf, and others have all been referred to at one time or another as critical architectures. Sometimes it is used as a vague term of respect, meaning something like a practice trying to do something serious, sometimes as an equally vague term of disrespect—referring to a practice whose only aspiration is to do something different.

As I suggested earlier, however indeterminate in architectural discourse, I believe that in every case one can trace a relationship between the term *critical* and the question of embodied meaning. From this point of view a critical architecture would be an architecture aspiring to participate in and arbitrate some debate by virtue of its ability to posit (or exemplify) one theoretical or critical position versus another. Though I myself doubt the very possibility of any architecture accomplishing such a task, in certain ways these uses of the notion of the critical appeal to common sense. What is wrong with the idea that some architectures can be distinguished from others by their aspiration and ability to stimulate intellectual and cultural discussion and that these therefore constitute a "critical architecture?"

As I have already suggested, one must consider that, like it or not, critical discourse has both a price and a politics. As James Mount, Atlanta's best-kept secret, writes, "Why do we have so much unrecognized talent? Why is there so much built crap displayed in the architectural press? . . . Why not cover the Dunseths, the Moroneys, the Curries . . . in Dothan and Natchez and New Orleans. [Their work] certainly cannot be as bad as . . . ."[3] The point is well taken: it is hard to believe that most of the critical architecture in the world is done by a few architects in a few cities. From my experience it is even harder to believe that the editors of the architecture press, including scholarly journals, are able and sufficient agents to determine criticality. Despite

4 William Homer,
Seurat and the Science of Painting
(Cambridge: MIT Press, 1964),
215–16.

5 Ibid.,
235.

an irrepressible desire for the contrary, criticism and marketing will always be co-implicated.

One must also consider the price and politics of silence. How does one weigh the tonnage of critical commentary stimulated by Eisenman's work against the silence that gathers around the work of, for example, Edward Larrabee Barnes, who is configured as the very exemplar of noncritical professional practice. Is there not always a great deal of critical content in conspicuous silence?

v   Rather than the politics of discourse or the content of silence, however, I am concerned with the very possibility of objects in general and architecture in particular operating critically. My claim is this: A notion of a critical architecture will always imply the possibility that a set of determinable meanings operate in the architectural object or, equivalently, that the proper context for the architectural object can always be determined. No doubt such a notion would allow for many meanings, operating at many different levels, from the programmatic to the formal to the symbolic to the theoretical to the ideological. But in any case, in order for the architecture to operate critically at all, in order, that is, for it to exemplify, participate in, and arbitrate a debate, any debate, it must be able to adjudicate, to yield some determinate meanings.

This principle goes well beyond the issue of symbolic signification. For example, in order for architecture to respond to the conclusions drawn from so-called rational methods, i.e., from histories, or from empirical or quantitative studies of architectural effects, design must be able to concretize those conclusions unambiguously and exclusively. Bubble diagrams and adjacency diagrams require not only that the rational intent, the "meaning" of the diagram, can be realized in the building but that the effects engendered by the building can be limited to that intent. There is no need to elaborate upon the unenviable history of that failed assumption.

Allow me to offer an anecdote to stage the problem as I see it. As was the case for most of his colleagues, the great French post-impressionist painter George Seurat was fascinated by the science of vision and hoped to respond in his paintings to a rigorous exploration of the relationships among vision, light, and painting. Indeed, Seurat was devoted to achieving a scientific rigor in his painting technique. He corresponded with leading scientists in the field, read their treatises, and strove to develop a technique that embodied the prevailing ideas about color vision. The result was his "pointillist" technique [c.]. The curious part of the story is that not only did Seurat misinterpret the theories, those theories were wrong. His painting method was derived from a misunderstanding of an incorrect theory! What conclusions can we draw? Can we say that if Seurat had correctly interpreted those incorrect theories, his paintings would have been better? Or that if the theories he studied had been correct, his paintings would have better still? No doubt every theorist whose work depends on a model of efficacious embodiment secretly wishes these non sequiturs were true.

Seurat's theory of painting was eclectic in nature and was based on a number of different sources rather than the ideas of a single writer or painter. . . . [And] these verbal and pictorial sources cannot be regarded as equally "scientific" in context.[4]

The Neo-Impressionist style Seurat created in 1884–1886 was not, as some writers have assumed, the result of slavishly following scientific treatises at the expense of visual perception of nature. . . . [H]is optical sensibilities were highly developed and . . . such texts served primarily to guide him in making his pictures operate according to the laws governing light and color in the physical world. . . . [O]ne of the most perplexing questions facing contemporary critics of Seurat's work concerned the degree to which he subordinated art to science.[5]

c.

6 Adolf Loos,
"Architecture," (1910)
in eds. Tim Benton and Charlotta Benton,
Architecture and Design: 1890–1939
(New York: Whitney Library of Design,
1975), 45.

Care is required here, however, for we must not underestimate the significance of Seurat's efforts to theorize his work. By virtue of theorizing Seurat recontextualized his painting, that is, he placed his painting technique in a dialogue with critical criteria different from those prevailing within the discipline of painting at that time.

On the one hand, prevailing disciplinary criteria are indispensable; they discipline the discipline. They provide the terms and conditions of an internal discourse, they enable an ongoing practice, they provide technique and a juridical environment and ultimately become the raw material for the transformation of the discipline. On the other hand, such criteria always behave as though they establish the complete constitutional discourse of a discipline, though in fact that discourse is never so much constitutional as institutional. The problem for both theorist and critic therefore can never be as simple as choosing sides between right and left, between elaborating upon the prevailing discourse and advocating new, outside influences. The problem is ceaselessly to renegotiate the unnegotiable tension between the two.

That Seurat's recontextualizing dialogue occurred across disciplinary boundaries was essential. The internal discourse of painting (as well as that of the science of vision) was loosened and transformed by virtue of that dialogue, and thus painting as a discipline was reconfigured to some extent, as were all of the other contexts in which painting participates, including, for example, the definition of the viewer. What did not occur was the dissolution of the disciplinary boundaries of painting, the subordination of painting to science as an application; whatever exchanges occur between painting and the science of vision, the latter will never stand as the master discourse of the other.

In one guise or another this story has been repeated countless times in art and architecture, though the number of its tellings has accelerated dramatically in the twentieth century. In a sense it is the general story of the encounter between disciplines and modernity, the latter understood as the scene of the failure to secure any master discourse (God, Man, Reason, Self, etc.) capable of organizing all discourses and providing an absolute context within which final critical and juridical decisions could occur.

Yet the lesson of such stories eludes the dominant trajectories of architectural theory and criticism. Astonishingly, within architectural criticism the two most suspicious arguments continue to retain their persuasive force, while the most reasonable garners the most suspicion. In the former, one hears that architecture is an autonomous discipline or that it should be subordinated to some other discourse. The first argues that architecture has its own history, principles, and logic and that the architect and the critic must confine themselves to those truths. Any effort to enter into a dialogue outside of those boundaries is fundamentally misguided or offers an analogy [d.]. The second

Only a very small part of architecture belongs to art: the tomb and the monument. Everything else, everything which serves a purpose should be excluded from the realms of art. . . . If we find a mound in the forest, six foot long and three foot wide, formed into a pyramid shape by a shovel, we become serious and something within us says, "Someone lies buried here." This is architecture.[6]

d.

7 See Jeffrey Kipnis,
"Freudian Slippers, or What are we to make of the fetish,"
in *Fetish*, ed. Greg Lynn, Edward Mitchell, Sarah Whiting
(New York: Princeton Architectural Press,
forthcoming in 1992).

8 Le Corbusier,
Towards a New Architecture,
trans. Frederick Etchells
(New York: Dover, 1986 [1923]),
14–15.

argues that the rationale for architectural design must be put on firmer ground, i.e., subordinated to or dissolved into some master discourse [e.]. Engineering, social science, business, philosophy, city planning, and history are just a few of the disciplines that at one time or another have been proposed as sufficient examples for architecture to follow. Why does everyone want to make an example of architecture?

Whatever their differences, both positions aspire to an architecture that embodies meaning and therefore require that architecture be capable of embodying meaning. Yet no object, no text, no architecture can fulfill such a requirement. That different contexts always supplement architecture and always engender different meanings from it, indicates that decisive embodiment as such cannot be achieved.[7]

The alternative attitude derives from the fact that architecture is an authentic discipline, yet one in continuous transformation. These transformations follow no particular trajectory nor do they serve any particular purpose. They result from the recontextualizing force of shifts in emphasis, of provisional framings of one or another of the many co-constructive dialogues that architecture constantly conducts with others.

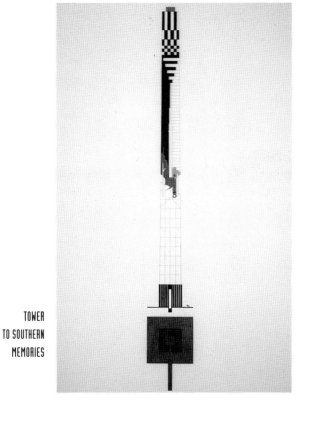

TOWER
TO SOUTHERN
MEMORIES

This position holds that architecture never embodies meaning but that, in concert with a particular decision context, it engenders meaning. As the same building participates in shifting contexts, it engenders shifting, even contradictory meanings. The aspiration that emerges from this position can be stated as DISGUISE: DELIMIT [to be read out loud]. Such an aspiration cannot lead to a critical architecture.

VI   If we take a quick look at some of the early individual competition entries by Elam and Scogin, we see clear examples of each of their initial flirtations with embodied meaning.

In Elam's entry for the "Tower to Southern Memories" competition she writes a history and future of Southern race relations, skillfully indenturing both the surface and the form of the tower

Our engineers are healthy and virile, active and useful, balanced and happy in their work. Our architects are disillusioned and unemployed, boastful or peevish. This is because there will soon be nothing more for them to do. *We no longer have the money* to erect historical souvenirs. At the same time, we have got to wash! Our engineers provide for these things and they will be our builders. . . . The diagnosis is clear. Our engineers produce architecture, for they employ a mathematical calculation which derives from natural law, and their works give us the feeling of HARMONY. The engineer therefore has his own Æsthetic, for he must, in making his calculations, qualify some of the terms of his equation; and it is here that taste intervenes. Now, in handling a mathematical problem, a man is regarding it from a purely abstract point of view, and in such a state, his taste must follow a sure and certain path.[8]

e.

9 Mack Scogin and Chuck Clark, from the Fort Lauderdale project description.

10 Ibid.

to her symbolic program. The notations on the vertical ascent of the tower represent the stages of this history: the suppression of the negroes, the escalating conflict resulting in the War Between the States, the subsiding of hostilities, gradual integration, and, ultimately, unity in the absence of race consciousness. The steps coalesce in an archetypal monumental totality.

Though literal in its symbolic aspirations, Elam's entry remains devoted to the reduced language of architectural abstraction. With but a few understated exceptions, it avoids explicit nonarchitectural figuration as much as possible in favor of reshuffling a reduced language of building to achieve its symbolic ends. Even the more figurative aspects of the work, the cracked masonry and exposed "artery," can be completely understood within architectonics. That Peter Eisenman, perhaps today's most outspoken advocate of a critical architecture defined as an architecture that embodies new meanings, awarded this project first place should not be ignored.

In Scogin's entry for the Fort Lauderdale public square competition [f.], he reveals an entirely different disposition. The design consists primarily of a topiary garden of popular culture symbols à la Venturi, organized by a somewhat vertiginous grid. Equal emphasis, however, is on program and in this sense Scogin evidences interest in the Parc de La Villette proposal of Rem Koolhaas in which there is no architecture proper; rather the entire proposal concerns the possibility of engendering a contemporary social field by the staged superposition of simultaneous events. Scogin too deemphasizes architecture proper in favor of ornament and staged event: "The drawings are conceptual sketches intended to convey the spirit of the ideas as well as the programmatic application of the design solution. Plans and elevations can be expected to evolve considerably when work begins." 9

The differences in the architectural personalities of Elam and Scogin suggested by these entries are worth another moment's

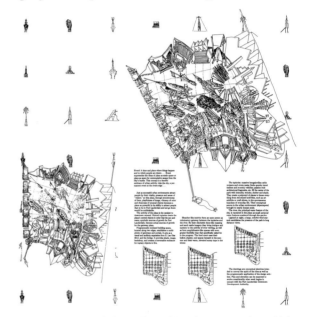

Event! A time and place where things happen and to which people are drawn. . . . Event supercedes the ideas of plaza as static space or plaza as space for contemplative escape from the city's bustle. This concept is a fanciful embrace of urban activity. Like the city, a permanent event at the river's edge. Just as successful urban environments attract people by their vitality, presence and sense of "object," so this plaza, through inventiveness of form, playfulness of image, vibrancy of color and closeness of unusual objects becomes a place so powerful that to not go there would be unthinkable.

The *topiaries*: massive bougainvillea cabin cruisers and crows nests; limbo gumbo travel trailers and re-entry vehicles; passion fruit architectural fragments, etc. fill the center of the park with intensity, wonder, shelter and shade. Bleacher-like *teatrino* form an open screen as culminatory gateway between the topiaries and the river. By their climbable dune-like massing and sand castle imagery they bring intrigue and mystery to the activity of river viewing, as well as form amphitheatre-like spaces with even greater flexibility than that specifically called for in the program. The river, the principal water feature of the city, is repeated in the plaza as small personal water features scattered through the garden. Lighted at night, a large colorful wind star-sock establishes the presence of the park in long distance views.

The drawings are conceptual sketches intended to convey the spirit of the idea . . .10

f.

**SCOGIN
SKETCH**

attention. Elam, ever the architect's architect, remains rigorous in her coordination of meaning, material, and form in a consistent architectural unity. Scogin, on the other hand, is eclectic, drawing effortlessly from disparate architectures with conflicting critical positions. Without much regard for their original declared purpose, Scogin sutures together disjointed ideas and forms according to his own idiosyncratic ends, an inclination more than suggested by his transmographic doodles.

One might speculate that the idiom emerging in the work of Scogin Elam and Bray consists at least in part of the inaudible conversation between these two dispositions, a conversation that doubtlessly occurs beyond the earshot even of the architects themselves. More importantly, I mention this because as we proceed to question the idea of a critical architecture further, we must also question how closely tied the notion is to the romantic myth of the architect as a heroic individual realizing a single-minded vision in design.

Whatever their differences, however, both entries clearly share the desire to embody meaning and can be situated in the reexamination of architectural meaning that has characterized design discourse over the last thirty years. In yet one more digression I would like quickly to review some of the key moments in that discourse in terms of my earlier discussion.

VII   I claim no historical or developmental foundation for the following theorems, which constitute the Three Masterpieces of Late Twentieth-Century Design Theory. Nor do I attribute them to the actual thoughts or intentions of the architects; the names indicate the architects whose work I believe most clearly supports the underlying conjecture.

The first is Rossi's Theorem, or the Architectural Memory Theorem, which says that the minimum element of architectural meaning is greater than and irreducible to its geometric constituents [g.]. This has probably been the most influential thought on architectural meaning of the second half of the twentieth century. Not only did it open the way to both the postmodernisms and studies of typology that dominated the last two decades, it raised the issue of the agendas that operated in modernism's reduction of architecture to programmed geometry. Finally, it mounts a powerful theoretical resistance to the tendency to subordinate architecture to any other discipline.

g.

Next we have Hejduk's Theorem, or the Theorem of Architectural Poetry, which says that the minimum unit of architectural poetry is greater than and irreducible to architectural memories [h.]. Closely aligned to Rossi's Theorem, this theorem nevertheless asserts the role of a dialogue with other discourses as essential to architecture. Although it stipulates the formal language of Rossi's Theorem and its criticism of modernism, it exposes and criticizes the stultifying reification of architecture's internal discourse implied by Rossi's Theorem.

Finally, Eisenman's Hypothesis, or the Hypothesis of Architectural Calculus, holds that minimum geometric, mnemonic, and poetic architectural configurations are all special cases of architecture conceived as a generalized calculus of meaning-embodying form [i.]. Noticing an artificial decision frame operating in the previous theorems, Eisenman's Hypothesis moves to correct them by pointing out the culturally determined predispositions they assert, which are not necessarily fundamental to architectural design. In particular, Eisenman's Hypothesis notices that the diagrams of the two previous theorems, to achieve their respective meanings, must take for granted the context of orientation established by an implied ground line. They both depend on conventions of scale: the figures are larger than the operators (+,<) and therefore do not enter into formal relationships with them. By detaching the aspects of the diagrams from their obligation to these decision rules, i.e., from a determining context, Eisenman's Theorem finds new formal relationships and therefore new possibilities for embodying meaning. Particularly, by rotating the geometric figures away from their ground plane orientation and by rotating and increasing the size of the plus-sign operator, an entirely new formal relationship can be discovered—one that, by the way, is a diagram of Eisenman's Wexner Center! At the Wexner Center, of course, Eisenman employed precisely such a calculus to write in the building a fictional account of the site's history and archaeology.

For our purposes, what is interesting about all three theorems is that in each case a proposition about architectural meaning operates to select one decision frame and to suppress another, a selection overturned and recontextualized in the next theorem. Let us speculate that the aspiration for a critical architecture is born from the fact that the architectural object always engenders a determined meaning when considered in any and every decision frame. And from the fact that it participates many decision frames, even those that produce contradictory and mutually exclusive determinations, the fulfillment of a critical architecture is fundamentally deferred.

VIII   In these terms consider again Elam's drawing for the tower. If we activate another context in which the proposal participates, e.g., if we take as the proposal the entire drawing and not simply the tower, what meaning are we to read into the white background that dominates the scheme? If we insist that the appropriate frame be the actual social space of the site, what then of other races? Elam takes up the difficult problem of architecture, undecidability, and meaning explicitly

h.

i.

11 Merrill Elam,
    from the Parking Lot
    project description.

in her proposal for a parking lot [j.]. A closer study of her proposal text confirms that Elam's idea is quite sophisticated. By grafting together two disjunctive elements, a banal parking lot and an enigmatic, beautifully detailed sculptural X, Elam hopes to set into motion a system capable of engendering many meanings as the context of its interpretation shifts. X is a symbol for the unknown, for "marking the spot," for multiplication, for rejections—"a symbol for fire, the rubbing of two sticks together . . . energy . . . linked conditions. . . ."[11] Thus as it hovers over the crass parking lot (designed, by the way, to emphasize its ordinariness,) the x affirms our love of the car while rejecting its pernicious consequences. Mounted on adjustable supports, even the location of the x is indeterminate. Indeed, as one contemplates the proposal, its meanings do proliferate.

As a realized scheme, however, the results would be somewhat disappointing. The project fails to insist upon the dislocating force of the graft [k.]; the two elements are content to remain unengaged. In part this occurs because the two elements do not problematize the classical structure of decidability that takes form variously as simple arrangements of inside/outside, structure/ornament, or decoration/function. Thus as a construction it might submit to recontextualization, although without the accompanying text it would not force the issue. Recalling my earlier remarks on the differences between buildings and projects, let us note that all of the subversive energy here is in the three-element project (X, parking lot, text), a system not dominated by presence and that cannot be ordered by the classical architecture of the structured pair or dialectic.

This study is intended to question the stereotyped habits of the mind. In the exercise common sense is defied; our common place knowledge of the parking lot is challenged. It is the unexpected that provides information. Meta-reality is evoked by the combination of familiar and extraordinary elements (objects, surfaces, spaces, etc.) in such a way that something unfamiliar is achieved. It is this unfamiliar aspect that transforms the parking lot and opens it to further consideration and contemplation.

The solution is a combination of an ordinary parking lot and an extraordinary x. The x is an expedient which carries us from the ordinary parking lot to some other reality. The juncture of the two elements, the x and the parking lot, seem to be obscurely attached or related by force of their natures and the multiple readings inherent in them. For example, the parking lot is loved for its convenience and hated for its visual impact; the x is a mark of rejection or the signifier of a very important place.

The parking lot is ordinary. It is made of asphalt paving with painted stripes. It is surrounded by standard issue sidewalks. It is utilitarian in intent.

The x is the opposite. It is smooth and finely detailed, striving for perfection. A structural frame is surrounded in a reflector-like material. During the day light glints off its surface. At night the x glows from within. At its support points the height of the x can be varied from time to time so that it unexpectedly acquires a new relationship to the horizontal surface of the parking lot. The x implies the boundaries of the parking lot and provides a frame that orders the space.

PLATTUS *I'm interested in work that offers a certain resistance to the kit of parts, tools, that I already have as a critic and as a historian; otherwise, I don't move forward. Jeff used the metaphor of grafting, and sometimes one's interested in rejections of grafts as well, and the kind of immune reactions where the fit's not accurate. One of the reasons why I was intrigued by the Chamber of Commerce building, given the general interest I have in the problem of difference in cultural criticism (which could have applied to almost anything), is because it made you work a little bit. At one level it was so obvious and at another level it was not obvious at all, unlike the Chmar House, which is a tour de force. I think it's a spectacular project. But from the modest point of view that I was trying to advance, it's pretty literal. The volumetric confrontation of those two pieces and the emphasis of those gaps between them is precisely about that stuff. It is almost an illustration of certain theoretical preoccupations. It lends itself to this role spectacularly well, which makes me a little bit more suspicious, or at least more intrigued by other things that don't immediately fit into the categories that I and others have created.*

The role of play in the parking lot and in Scogin's Fort Lauderdale scheme should not be underestimated, however. Play-as-such is the activation of an object's undecidability, its participation in many contexts. Play therefore subverts criticality, and the

j.   k.

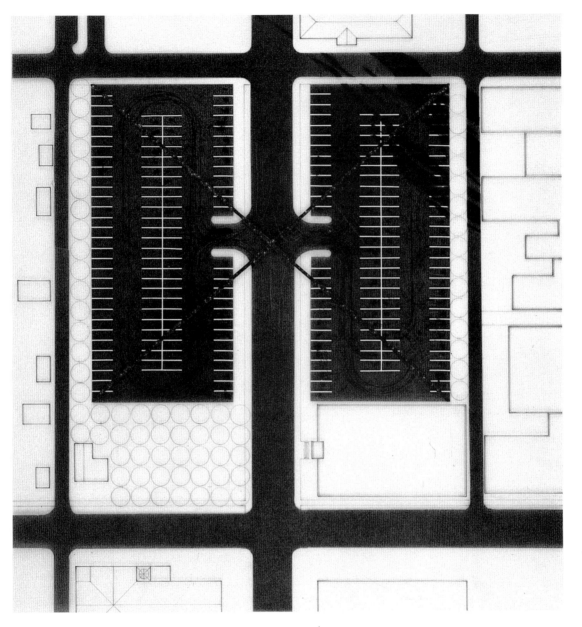

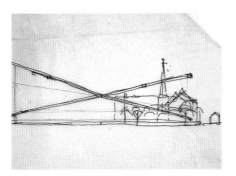

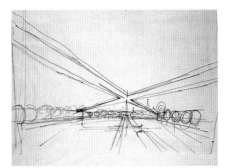

12 Immanuel Kant,
    Critique of Judgement,
    trans. J. H. Bernard
    (New York: Hafner Press,
    1951 [1790]),
    61 (§14).

13 Jacques Derrida,
    "Structure, Sign and Play
    in the Discourse of the Human Sciences"
    in *Writing and Difference*, trans. Alan Bass
    (Chicago: University of Chicago Press,
    1978 [1967]), 289.

14 Georges Bataille,
    "Post-Scriptum" in *L'expérience intérieure*
    (Paris: Gallimand, 1943).
    [Quoted in Jacques Derrida,
    "From Restricted to General Economy,"
    Writing and Difference, 335.]

44

CHILDREN'S
GALLERY,
ATLANTA
HIGH MUSEUM

irrepressible possibility of play guarantees that in the end criticality cannot be achieved [l.]. Indeed, play is of the essence in the work of Scogin Elam and Bray, and any criticism of the work that fails to take play into account is congenitally suspect.

Thus serious attention must be paid when, while at Heery & Heery, Scogin, Elam and others took up the problem of play in their installations for the children's gallery at Atlanta's High Museum. I am curious if these "non-serious" works could ever qualify as critical architecture. Biographical critics of Scogin Elam and Bray should look to these installations not only for their anticipation of the firm's indulgence in play but for their team approach to the design process.

Play is evident even in a "serious" work such as the High Museum at Georgia Pacific Center. Its most important spatial device is a play upon the provisionally objective framing capabilities of section versus the totalizing, critical neutrality established by the plan. The simple binuclear plan of

Every form of the objects of sense (both of external sense and also mediately of internal) is either *figure* or *play*. In the latter case it is either play of figures or (in space, viz. pantomime and dancing) of the mere play of sensations (in time).[12]

Totalization . . . is sometimes defined as *useless*, and sometimes as *impossible*. . . . Totalization can be judged impossible in the classical style: one then refers to the empirical endeavor of either a subject or a finite richness which it can never master. There is too much, more than one can say. But nontotalization can also be determined in another way: no longer from the standpoint of a concept of finitude as relegation to the empirical, but from the standpoint of the concept of *play*.[13]

Only the serious has *a meaning*: play, which no longer has one, is serious only in the extent to which "the absence of meaning is also a meaning," but is always lost in the night of an indifferent nonmeaning.[14]

the "building" is thoroughly subordinated to the frame-in-a-frame-in-a-frame sectional layering. Throughout the procession from the main building to the museum, the visitor sees first the entire gallery, then the art and other visitors momentarily framed by the architecture, as are they themselves glimpsed by others. Thus long before the visitor arrives in the gallery space the critical objectivity and distance sought by the frames and pedestals of the art and promised by the plan has been subverted by the picture-framing sequence in architectural space. And, given the photo supplied by the architect, can one be sure that the geometry of the barrel vault is not derived from Scogin's forehead?

HIGH MUSEUM AT GEORGIA PACIFIC CENTER

15 Sigmund Freud,
The Interpretation of Dreams,
trans. James Strachey
(New York: Avon, 1965 [1900]),
545–46.

CODEX
COMPETITION
ENTRY

I would like to close with a brief discussion of one of my personal favorites among contemporary architectural projects, the extraordinary Codex Competition entry produced by Mack Scogin, Chuck Clark, Steve Swicegood, Merrill Elam, Wylie Gaston, and Susan Desko while at Heery & Heery. I had the privilege of exhibiting this proposal in my art gallery in Atlanta, and it has remained in my mind ever since. All of the ingredients that threaten critical architecture are magnificently choreographed here. While in no way derivative, it is eclectic beyond belief, collaging the conspicuous influence of such architects as Graves, Rossi, Gehry, Eisenman, and even Leon Krier. The stylistic chaos alone is dizzying.

The play technique in the design process is best described in Freud's description of the dream-work [m.], and the result is nightmarish architecture. Not quite commensurate four-square, nine-square, and sixteen-square organizations are superimposed, so that center and hierarchy are constantly promised then deferred. Diagramming the project would be much like diagramming one of Faulkner's three-page sentences. Plays on words become form as the "isolatrium" provides a second primary entry. Unlike the honorific entry, which marks a dialectic threshold from outside to inside, passage through trees in the isolatrium introduces a third outside-inside space, a curtain raising, a solipsistic caesura between the public out-

The dream has above all to avoid censorship, and with that end in view the dream-work makes use of a *displacement of psychical intensities* to the point of a transvaluation of all psychical values. The thoughts have to be reproduced exclusively or predominantly in the material of visual and acoustic memory-traces, and this necessity imposes upon the dream-work *considerations of representability* which it meets by carrying out fresh displacements. . . . Little attention is paid to the logical relations between the thoughts; those relations are ultimately given a disguised representation in certain *formal* characteristics of dreams.[15]

m.

side and the collective inside [n.].

Elsewhere, at Elam's tower, for example, I have used the technique of including the representation of the project as the project to effect a reframing. In this scheme the team takes that technique to a vertiginous limit. The scheme is doubled and reiterated again and again in the four-, nine-, and sixteen-square groupings of the presentation panels. The model becomes an episode in the drawing, an egg becomes the isolatrium; vitamin pills and rubber bands become God knows what. One cannot find any single thing that can confidently be called "the scheme." Which brings us to the last threat to critical architecture that I will mention today: team design, the genuine amalgam of personalities, tendencies, and ideas through play. Important in the children's galleries, fundamental to Codex, the destabilizing effect of team design continues to color the work of Scogin Elam and Bray today.

Clearly, I have not even begun a sober criticism of the Codex scheme. But, in closing, I should not leave the impression that if I had time, I could do so. Of course, I could catalogue in detail many more features of the project.

The design solution presented here amplifies Codex's interest in its headquarters site, that is, the headquarters complex is an extension of the farm complex. Instead of separating themselves from the farm building, the new buildings engage the old, drawing the older ambiance into the new, and easing the new into the old.

The diversity and choice of forms, views and vistas create a complex environment which piques the creative mind. There is no centrality; hierarchy is embodied in activity, not the architecture. The activities are clearly categorized as "on" and "off"; work and play; creation and recreation. The "on" spaces are efficient machines for serving the needs of the user and the "off" spaces are determined by the desire for less structured creation and recreation.

At the transition between the old and new, the laboratory building symbolizes the balance of tradition of the existing (the farm side) and the fantasy of the future (the new side). The activity it houses is research of precedent, and formulation of the ideal; the result being realistic innovation.

The office building sits firmly on the ground establishing stability and edge. It protects and forms a backdrop for the entry court as seen through the filter of the laboratory piloti. Similarly it creates an edge to the meadow which contains the isolatrium.

The isolatrium is an unprogrammed element which is representational of the future new life style of Codex. Opportunities to pass through it at the beginning of each day are present, as it is situated above the protected parking decks. It instills the spirit of the complex to the employee traveling to his or her workstation and its oasis-like qualities provide a place for reflective thought and creation.

This environment, generated by the objectives of the ultimate users of the site, is created through the presence of choice, diversity and unity; ambiguity within an overall clarity. These qualities are those in which the intellectual pursuit of creation can take place. [16]

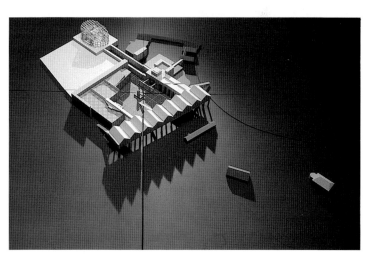

CODEX
COMPETITION
ENTRY

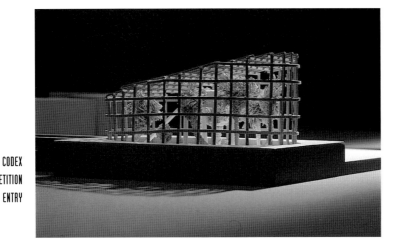

CODEX
COMPETITION
ENTRY

Its site strategies and programming, for example, are simply bizarre, although, like the rest of the scheme and like a dream, they somehow make perfect sense. I have returned to this project again and again, wondering if some new insight, some new language, some newly acquired analytic skill or technique would clarify it for me once and for all, always to no avail.

What is this project? A tour de force of sleights of hand, tricks, lies, false promises, illusions, and grotesque syntheses, all wrapped in a visage of architectural courtesy and good will. Its very virtue is that it is not a critical architecture, nor will it ever deliver itself to architectural criticism. To my mind, the enigma of Codex proves that however fascinating and important the effort to secure a critical architecture is, the effort to subvert it will always be more important. Why? Because in its success the former kills architecture, while the latter keeps its alive.

NEW VISIONS GALLERY

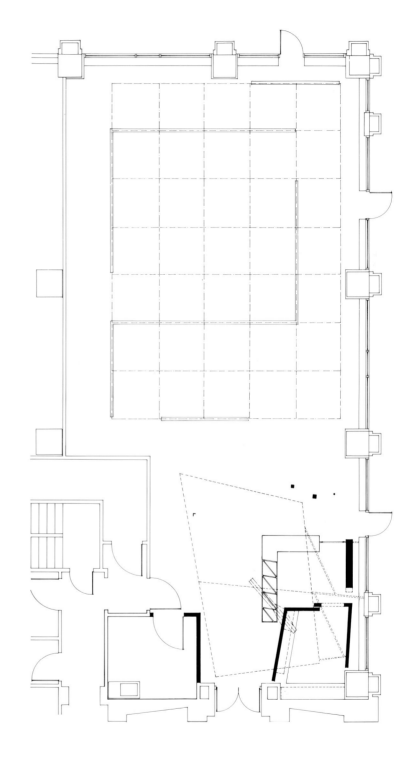

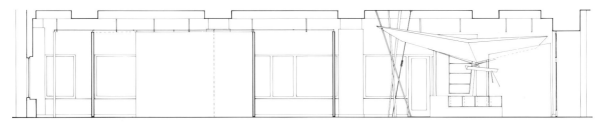

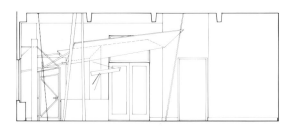

CHMAR HOUSE

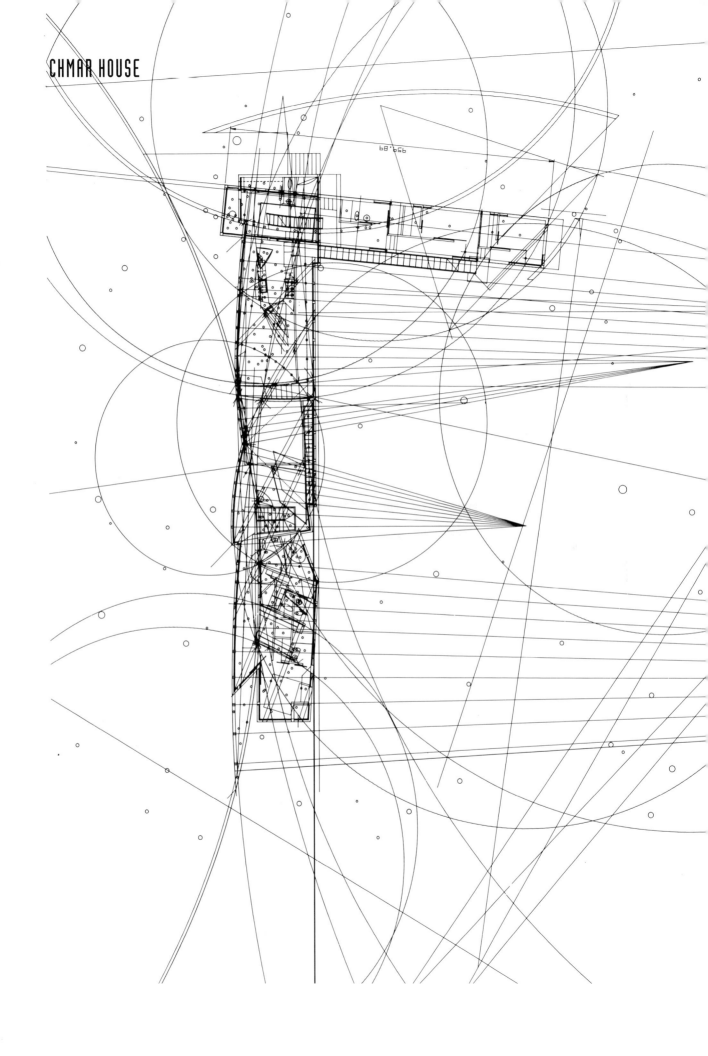

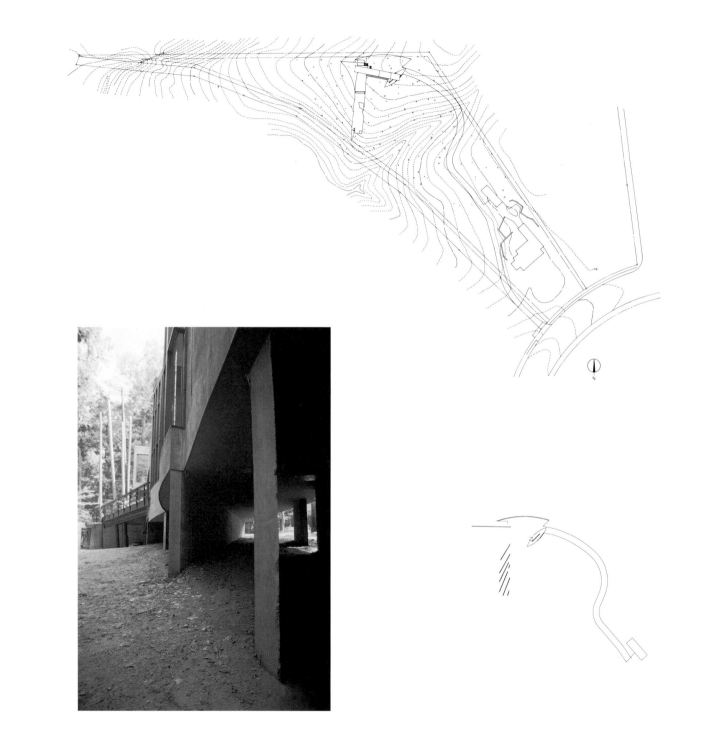

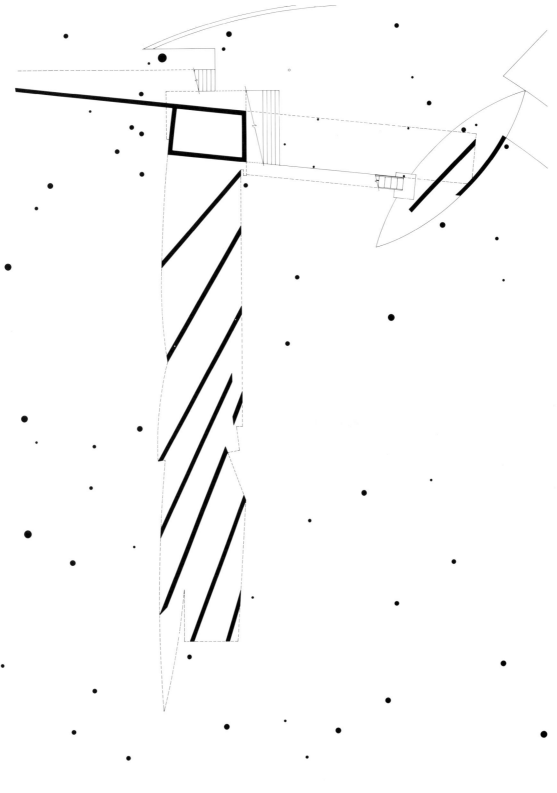

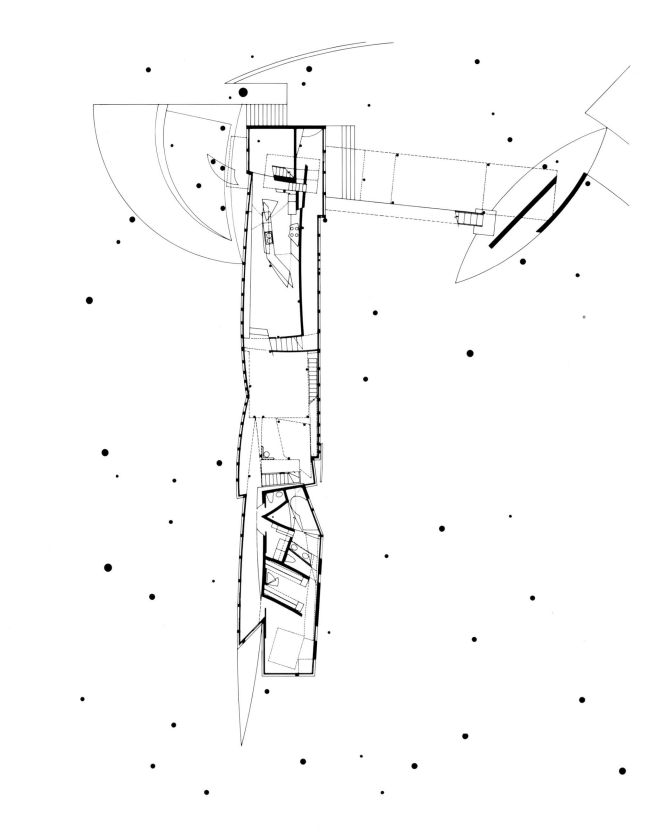

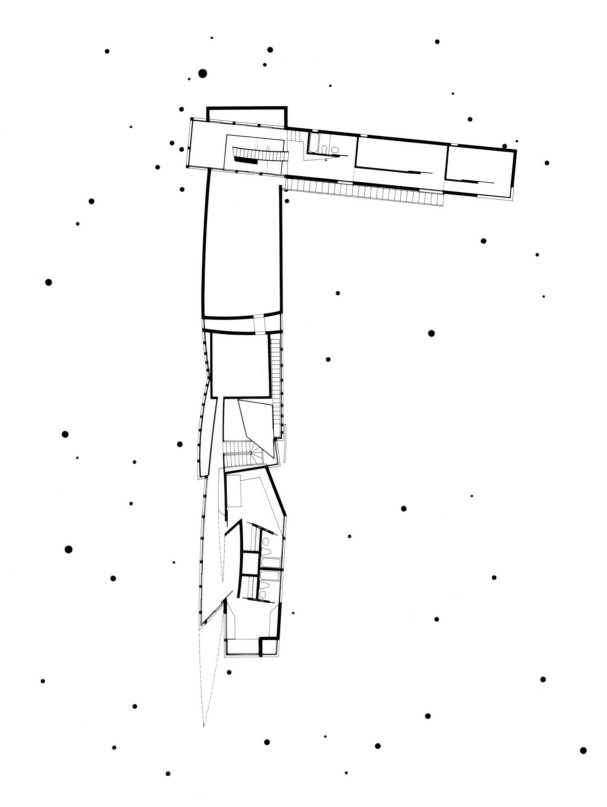

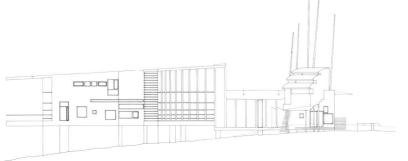

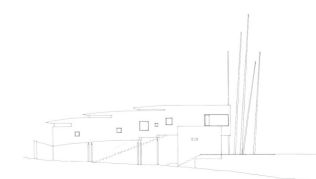

Building a Practice: Scogin Elam and Bray and Social Space

Jennifer Wicke

[1] Andrea Kahn, "The Invisible Mask" in *Drawing/Building/Te.* (New York: Princeton Architectural Press, 1991 86.

What distinguishes even the worst of architects from the best of bees, as Marx famously pointed out, is that architects erect structures in the imagination before giving them material form. Holding the imaginative structure poised for scrutiny on the very verge of materialization is architecture's unique contribution to the theoretical; this double instantiation is found nowhere else in the aesthetic or cultural realm and gives architecture its particular cast: a building has a shadowy life as a structure of visual and verbal imagination simultaneous with its builtness, its concrete existence. An important theoretical juncture of the last several years, intersecting with architectural practice and architectural criticism, has to do with how the unique status of the architectural artifact interpenetrates the theoretical enterprise itself, from the vantage of those who are not architects and are not working within the specific discourse of architecture criticism. A certain allegorization of architecture invests theory's more local preoccupations now; the architectural building, both as unrealized mental structure and as materialized emblem, has come to symbolize, or allegorize, various abstract states or conditions within theory itself, as if individual buildings were playing roles in an allegorical theater staged by theory. In extra-architectural theory, if the realms can be starkly differentiated for a moment, architecture has come to stand in for the contradictions of theory or current cultural predicaments; in intra-architectural theory the allegory of architecture often remains invisible [a.]. This strategic place for architecture on the critical scene suggests that an assessment of the movement between theory and architecture might reveal new directions for critical thought and practice; in particular, the work of Scogin Elam and Bray elides the "allegorical" in crucial and even elegant ways.

Ever since Fredric Jameson staggered through John Portman's Bonaventure Hotel in Los Angeles [b.] and called it an experience of the "hyperspace of postmodernity," the need to articulate the dwelling of the postmodern has been acute, and architecture and architectural references have been central to giving this reality its habitation and its name. Despite its shortcomings, *postmodernism* lingers as the name for the contemporary theoretical moment and must be deployed here as a way of imperfectly identifying an inescapable frame for critical discussion. Clearly, postmodernism in such a context does not refer to the specifics of a "postmodern" architectural style, now superseded or outmoded in any event, but rather to the loose and baggy monster of postmodern thought, which moves in iceberg fashion across the sea of our disciplines, revealing only its tantalizing tip and thereby asserting the importance of what has yet to be formulated. In this use, postmodernism is a more capacious term than *post-structuralism* with its very particular references. *Theory* is problematized too, since its parameters are also shifting and vague and its reification as a single monolith is erroneous. Because my use of these terms is necessarily somewhat slapdash, I must point out that *theory* is often shorthand for *critical theory*, a term with a much more satisfactory

To look past is at once to see past—in the sense of overlooking or dismissing. This oversight of architecture's political effects allows for unwitting acceptance of, or submission to, a controlling power hidden or enclosed within the readily seen. To discern this power one must attend to the invisible in architecture.[1]

b.   a.

2 Mike Davis,
"Urban Renaissance and
the Spirit of Postmodernism,"
New Left Review 151 (1985):
112.

genealogy. *Critical* theory is implicit in the following discussion of the vagaries of postmodern theory's collision with the architectural, and architectural criticism or critique hides behind the somewhat more expedient phrase *architectural theory*. The *critical* in critical theory is key to this argument, because the theoretical innovations of Scogin Elam and Bray have to do with articulating a thoroughly critical practice of architecture.

Jameson's somewhat hyperbolic enthrallment with the Bonaventure was nonetheless a galvanizing moment, seized upon in numerous commentaries on his seminal essay "Postmodernism: The Cultural Logic of Late Capitalism" [c.]. One explanation for this flurry of interest is that here Jameson enacted the very allegorization of architecture so alluring to postmodern theorists of whatever critical stripe—a single building as emblem of a theoretical riddle that was also a feature of everyday life, its "hyperspace." Various critics retorted that Portman's hotel was anything but postmodern, that it was the last relic of high modernism or a final gasp of suburban mall-ery, in Mike Davis's words, "a vivarium for the upper-middle class,"[2] and that the ineffabilities of hyperspace that Jameson attributed to its dizzying reflective surfaces and obscured entries and exits had more to do with quite effable strategies for keeping a surrounding ethnic neighborhood at bay. How could Jameson get the building so wrong, in short, using this architectural experience as a kind of shorthand analogue for the vertiginous spaces of postmodernity in general? Was it a failure of taste or a failure of nerve that led him to designate the architectural valence of the postmodern at such a quaint remove from the subtlety of the rest of his speculations? More importantly, despite the criticisms lodged against this feature of his argument, why did the architecture itself capture the attention and crystallize the response to Jameson's essay? The textual fetishization of the architectural artifact in current theory, in other words, its allegorization, is symptomatic of a theoretical and cultural predicament that Jameson demonstrates and we, as his readers, enact.

The choice of building would not matter much (and in the ultimate scheme of things does not matter much), except that it points to a kind of break in the neat picket fence of discursive formation: architecture crops up in the theoretical forms as an exemplary mode, as an object of commentary, as an allegory, but not as a practice or process. The singular artifact, the building, completed and iconic, is isolated and criticized, or woven in, or used illustratively in formulating an allegory of the theoretical scene, instead of directing the same critical energy to understanding the interstitial web surrounding the single, flamboyant building, instead of demarcating the movements and practices of buildings in relation to their sites and to the conditions of their builtness. Jameson, for example, uses the Bonaventure Hotel as exemplary text on a par with his mordant assessment of Andy Warhol's *Diamond Dust Shoes*, and with an analysis of the film *Body Heat*. Architecture as a practice, even as a critical practice, is not figured in; architecture remains a static *figure*, an allegory of

This essay has taken several forms; the first incarnation was published as "Postmodernism and Consumer Society" in *The Anti-Aesthetic*, ed. Hal Foster (Port Townsend, Wash.: Bay Press, 1983), in a later version as "Postmodernism: The Cultural Logic of Late Capitalism" in *New Left Review* 146 (July–August 1984), and in a further one as "Postmodernism and Consumer Society" in *Postmodernism and its Discontents*, ed. E. Ann Kaplan (New York: Verso, 1988).

c.

itself, a figural motif in the larger tapestry of theory. This is less a result of the inevitable widespread ignorance of architecture as a discipline and a process in its own right than a manifestation of disturbances within theory, which architectural criticism then echoes.

If there is a problem in devoting adequate critical attention to the social and historical, the processual and the spatial aspects of architecture within theory generally, and within architectural criticism at times, this reflects critical impasses that have invaded theory *tout court*. In the theoretical wing of deconstruction, for example, the difficulty of getting at the social arises because the preoccupation with language, text, and rhetoric is incapable of accounting for the social and historical [d.]. Nothing intrinsically prevents deconstructive theory from a concentration on social practices, but that is not the direction it has taken, and however productive and fruitful its gestures have been—immensely so, most would agree—the figural or allegorical tendencies within deconstruction have made it hard to move to contemplating social practices at large. No doubt this is a stark and rather reductive statement of the circumstances within theory today; nonetheless, it fairly represents the parameters of the discussion. Architectural criticism, where grafted onto this body of thought, most often (but of course, not exclusively) has adopted the Icarus wings of rhetorical analysis and become entranced with seeing individual buildings as hieroglyphs of language. This intensifies the building's singularity, as the building is seen to enact the unstable, indeterminate, self-cannibalizing aspects held to obtain for all language: theory is used to explain what the building design is an allegory of, or for, in a self-referential looping back to the building as emblem. The linguistic analogies between architecture and language are extremely rich, yet must be scanted here in favor of pointing out rather sharply how a figural approach to architectural building can lead to rather static illustrative architecture.

This critical paradox looks somewhat different from outside the precincts of architectural criticism, for one whose field is critical theory in the extended literary and cultural domain, not architectural criticism specifically; perhaps the most useful contribution from "outside" is to pose delicate questions across the turbulent and distended body of

PLATTUS *I think everybody used an abstract noun which they would have liked to make concrete, namely "politics." For lack of the intimate knowledge of the politics that make a place, one alludes to a desire to get more involved with that place. Criticism is probably inclined to be a little cool, and architecture as an activity, the practice of architecture, as Mack was saying, tends to be on the hot side whether you want it to be or not. You can't help but get totally enmeshed with the characters that make a place, the idiosyncracies of zoning law and the difference between one suburb and the next suburb. As an architect, you sometimes wish you could disentangle yourself from these things, but sometimes as a critic you wish you could find a way of entering into them because it heats up the criticism. I think everybody who spoke today would like to heat up criticism to make it more immediate and less abstract. In spite of the differences, I think there was a general tendency in that direction: not to abandon but, to qualify the structural and normative dimension of architectural language and to inject some element of the strategic, the opportunistic, the empirical, the casual, even the arbitrary: the things that animate a place and its events. So I wouldn't make the claim that I could be more rigorous about the work, but rather that I could be a little bit less abstract about it. If I knew a lot more about Merrill and Mack and Lloyd's work and a lot more about the special character of the places where it has existed and the circumstances under which it was made, those things would enrich each other.*

d.

3 Mary McLeod,
"Introduction,"
Architecture Criticism Ideology
(New York: Princeton
Architectural Press, 1985),
9–10.

4 Jeffrey Kipnis,
"Nolo Contendere,"
Assemblage 11
(April 1990):
57.

theory [e.]. This entails scattering some unwelcome rain on the parade of architectural criticism, because such queries address the lag in theoretical time that has allowed deconstruction to seem the *dernier cri* in that bandwagon, as it wanes and ebbs painfully on other fronts [f.]. The delay is not by any means simply a matter of fashion but rather has been fed by the allegorization of architecture—the turning of discrete buildings into figures or replications of theoretical conundrums— discernible in much post-structuralist theory; it also reflects the condition that Mary McLeod describes in this way:

> Although architecture of all the arts is most directly tied to economic and social conditions given both its scale of production and public use, the field contains almost no tradition outside the Soviet Union of Marxist criticism or Marxist avant-garde practice. During the thirties, when in the United States art historians such as Meyer Shapiro and Clement Greenberg, strongly influenced by Marxist theory, sought to reveal the ideological nature of painting and sculpture, no equivalent socially based criticism emerged in architecture. Even the Frankfurt School—Theodor Adorno, Max Horkheimer, Leo Lowenthal, Walter Benjamin, and Herbert Marcuse—largely ignored architecture. There exists no Marxist study devoted to architecture comparable in scope and quality to Lukacs's investigations of the novel or Adorno's analysis of music.[3]

One can immediately ask whether this void is as thoroughgoing as McLeod claims, since one can cite numerous examples of an emphasis on architecture within this body of thought. Walter Benjamin's now partially reconstructed Paris Arcades project is a compelling counter-example, but it has undoubtedly made it more possible for the predominantly textual modes of post-structuralism to take up lodging within architectural criticism, as if there were no other valences within such thought, and to persist there with the adhesion of the new long past its superannuation in other theoretical contexts. This is not to question theory's relevance or its role; on the contrary, it is to ask for more theory, for the opening up of more architectural terrain to theoretical scrutiny and, conversely, to ask that architectural criticism require more critical theory in its theorizations.

A second major reason for the lag exists on another front and is connected to the enormous resources of capital, pedagogy, and institutionalization obtaining in architecture and thus in criticism and theory. Literary theory, by contrast, travels relatively light; the volatility of its critical productions exacts little actual price, except in the arena of the reproduction of knowledge, whereas architectural theory is always interpenetrated with the commodified reality of building and thus is freighted by constraints on theoretical change and demands that it be persuasive to those who will underwrite the building in question. To translate a theoretical mode into a design practice involves massive financial commitments, efforts of public persuasion and

Deconstruction does not render works— artistic, political, social, philosophical, etc.— meaningless, despite the relentless efforts to characterize it as doing so. Nor does it dissolve the object. Though it does indeed subvert every analysis, theory, philosophy, or phenomenology of the object, and thus may be said to dissolve the "classical object," insofar as it articulates the inevitability and irrepressibility of framing it also maintains the object.[4]

WICKE *I prefaced my talk by saying that I am an interloper in the discourse but into the day I have had it conclusively demonstrated to me that this is exactly the discourse that we all share. There were no stark boundary lines, any barriers, to the permeabilities to these discourses and the projects: the question of difference, the notion of gender and architecture, the question about reformulating the notion of ornament and modernity, the question of excess and fetishism. That's the domain of theory. On one hand it surprised me and on the other hand it didn't surprise me at all. Why should it, because if one is assuming that cultural criticism broadly conceived has something to do with all of these matters then in fact it has proven itself to be just that.*

e.

f.

municipal lobbying, and the long *durée* of actual building time.

The successful transferral of the preoccupations of a primarily deconstructive postmodernism to architecture is in itself a fascinating ideological effect, symptomatic of the ahistoricity of architectural theorization, while the textuality of deconstruction genuinely offers a demystification of the objects of architecture and a rhetorical figuration for its insatiable formal appetite. In other words, while this analysis doesn't try to diminish the powerful value that deconstructive postmodernism had and has for architecture's theory and practice (the Wexner Center, Parc de la Villette, and other sites illustrate this potential), it simply questions why it seems to remain dominant there with a force absent elsewhere on the critical scene. To answer this question again requires an excursus into the shifting vagaries of postmodern theory itself.

To begin with the political and let that eddy out into the linguistic perimeters of the field: to an extent postmodern thought addresses a crisis in political representations, one that Jean-François Lyotard's formulation of the supersession of master-narratives in *The Postmodern Condition* has been taken to typify [g.]. The loss of the Enlightenment's *grand recits* (meta-narratives) of rational progress and teleological political transformation corresponds to the failure of universalizing discourses and authoritative programs, to which we might all accede. Ironically enough, post-structuralist theory, which seems to characterize postmodern discourse in much architectural critical writing, would exclude the postmodern itself as a condition or a period; Paul de Man's famous rejection of modernism in "Literary History, Literary Modernity," which declares that modernity is the moment of all literary periods since it is perpetually rediscovered to bracket the present from the past, is echoed in Lyotard's paradox that the postmodern precedes the modern, is the internalized moment that, in skirting the edge of sublime unrepresentability, permits the modern to be created. Lyotard's schismatic discourse announces itself as an encyclopedic offshoot of the Enlightenment by its very engagement with a historical episteme, only to deny this historicity by retreating to the aestheticization of the postmodern in what he calls the "Svelte Appendix," a paean to modernist art. History is posited but then evacuated on the grounds of theory, as myriad language games take the place of the conversation of the faculties, in Kant's more decorous language. Given with one hand, taken back with the other—in some ways, this theoretical sleight-of-hand mimics the ease with which architecture has evaded its own historicity, its own imbrication in the social, despite the ample empirical evidence one supposes is there to be mobilized.

To explore this lack requires entering a discourse that may, on the face of it, seem utterly tangential to the problems of architecture in this theoretical moment, or at least only abstractly related to the present inquiry, but that is ultimately quite relevant to placing the work of Scogin Elam and Bray outside the framework of allegory or textual figure. Space is in question here,

This seminal text
was first published
as *La condition post-
moderne* (Paris:
Minuit, 1979), and
then translated with
its "Svelte Appendix"
as *The Postmodern
Condition: A Report
on Knowledge*
(Minneapolis: University
of Minnesota, 1984).

g.

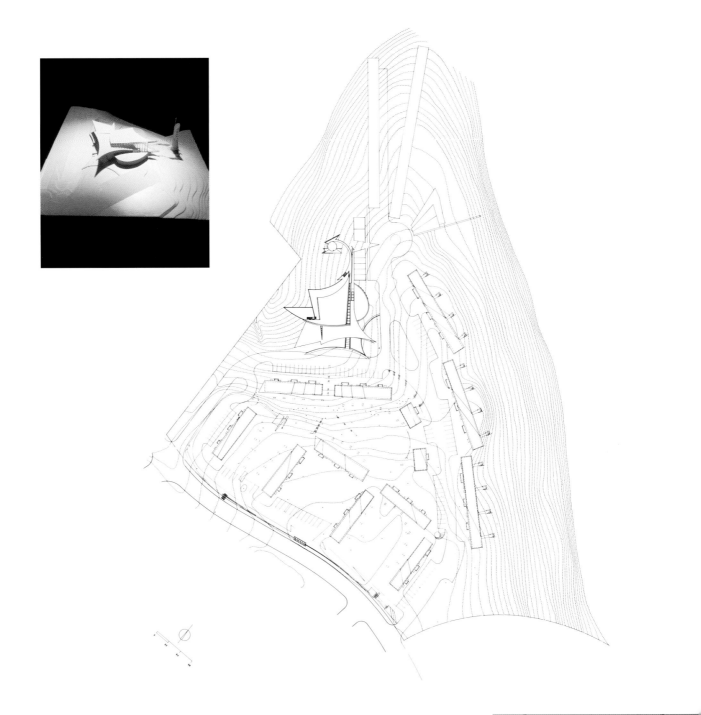

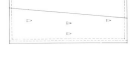

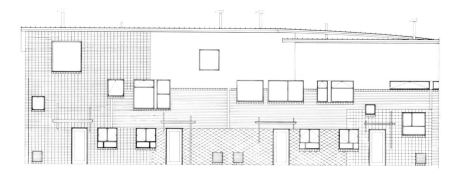

5 Ernesto Laclau and Chantal Mouffe,
Hegemony and Socialist Strategy
(New York: Verso, 1985),
142.

6 Michel Foucault,
*Discipline and Punish:
The Birth of the Prison,*
trans. Alan Sheridan
(New York: Vintage, 1979),
200.

7 Foucault,
Discipline and Punish,
205.

8 Robert Segrest,
"The Perimeter Projects:
Notes for Design,"
Assemblage 1 (November 1986):
25–26.

space as a discursive problem in social analysis [h.]. The social itself is most typically analogized or reified as a space, within which, then, the social proceeds to take place, as phrases like *the social realm* reveal. The theorization of social space begins to be a site within theory where the architectural has pride of place and where architectural criticism can offer a major contribution.

Assessing the social as a spatial formation usually means attempting to rearrange the counters of political discourse as well, and the recent theorists who have entered this fray are primarily critical theorists with Marxist or post-Marxist concerns. Important here are Ernesto Laclau and Chantal Mouffe, who have recently addressed the problematics of social space to account for "hegemony"—they follow Antonio Gramsci in so labeling the literal and the symbolic forces of the state—in a new way. They oppose the notions that the social space is the absolute centrality of power, with people sutured to the social along one axis of social logic, and that the social space is a diffuse setting of power relations.

> The problem of power cannot, therefore, be posed in terms of the search for the class or the dominant sector which constitutes the center of a hegemonic formation, given that, by definition, such a center will always elude us. But it is equally wrong to propose as an alternative, either pluralism or the total diffusion of power within the social, as this would blind the analysis to the presence of nodal points and to the partial concentrations of power existing in every concrete social formation.[5]

This last is a relatively unveiled critique of Foucault, who represents the social space as hinging on a panoptical eye from which radiate diffuse waves of power relations, untraceable back to their "source," or nodal point [i.]. Laclau and Mouffe want to keep the social space much more dynamic, turning it into a plurality of spaces resisting any total order.

> It is only when the open, unsutured character of the social is fully accepted, when the essentialism of the totality and of the elements is rejected, that this potential becomes clearly visible . . . these conditions arise originally in the field of what we have termed the democratic revolution, but they are only maximized in all their deconstructive effects in the project for a radical democracy, or, in other words, in the form of politics which is founded not upon dogmatic postulation of any "essence of the social," but, on the contrary, on affirmation of the contingency and ambiguity of every "essence," and on the constitutive character of social division and antagonism. Affirmation of a ground which lives only by negating its fundamental character; of an order which exists only as a partial limiting of disorder; of a meaning which is constructed only as excess and paradox in the face of meaninglessness—in other words, the field of the political as the

The panoptic mechanism arranges spatial unities that make it possible to see constantly and recognize immediately.[6]

The Panopticon . . . must be understood as a generalizable model of functioning; a way of defining power relations in terms of the everyday life of men. . . . The fact that it should have given rise, even in our own time, to so many variations, projected or realized, is evidence of the imaginary intensity that it has possessed for almost 200 years. But the Panopticon must not be understood as a dream building; it is the diagram of a mechanism of power reduced to its ideal form; its functioning, abstracted from any obstacle, resistance or friction, must be represented as a pure architectural and optical system; it is in fact a figure of political technology that may and must be detached from any specific use.[7]

In the wide space of architecture, that which is not the building is of no consequence. Ideas, descriptions, critiques, theories, even ideology—all abstractions—are, in the end, passive and inert, the ether of the architectural space. The object—separate and privileged—is the sole subject of an enclosed and centripetal order. Architecture is a collection of ruins that closes at six o'clock.

Or so the story has gone. . . . SPACE, not history, not time, is (still) the totalizing force in American experience. It has always been the case. . . . It is the landscape of the American imagination.[8]

i.   h.

9 Laclau and Mouffe,
Hegemony and Socialist Strategy,
192–93.

10 Robert Bocock,
Hegemony
(London: Ellis Horwood
& Tavistock, 1986),
63.

11 Bocock,
Hegemony,
63.

space for a game which is never "zero-sum," because the rules and the players are never fully explicit. This game, which eludes the concept, does at least have a name: hegemony[9] [j.].

One hears here the resonant echoes of much of the ground-clearing textual practice that appears under the heading of deconstruction—the elimination of a center, the undermining of binary oppositions and the dissolving of "essence," the negations built into the very originating concepts that mark out the field, and so on—the space to which Laclau and Mouffe refer could, under another guise, be read very well as the page, the textual page upon which the self-undoings of language perform their alchemies. Yet this analogy holds some peril for Laclau and Mouffe, and their reluctance to accept it is what separates this spatial discourse from the linguistic or rhetorical focus of deconstruction. For deconstruction, language is the determination of the social; in the materialist thought of Laclau and Mouffe and others, the situation is precisely the reverse: the social is that which determines language. In this reversal lies the world of difference that demarcates social space in the radical ways postmodernity suggests, with obvious implications for architecture. A concentration on social space invokes social relations, an energized field linking building to building, surely, but also placing buildings within practices of social relation. Architectural criticism's encounters with theory have often exacted a price for the predominance of text and writing as models for discourse. The powerful negative critique of deconstruction, for example, is its claim that the explosion of order, origin, and authority occurs within language and that the de-construction of language involves subverting the assumptions of logic and rationality at their roots in language. Attention to the constructive, all-embracing nature of language is the hallmark of twentieth-century theory and a crucial insight in all its variants. Nonetheless, to rhetoricize or textualize totally the theoretical terrain of architecture runs the risk of limiting critique to very strict textual barriers. Deconstruction has, for literary theory, offered an etiolated version of the page in favor of language engaged as the social; its transfer over to architecture has at times been equally restrictive, and nowhere more so than in the failure to engage with social space. If architecture wants to narrow its transgressive theoretical arena to that of text, it will inevitably invoke the allegory of the (single) building instead of the building as a practice in social space, because architectural practice will be seen as tantamount to writing out in material form the blockages or impasses, the allegories, of inscribed forms or written language. Hegemony inevitably will be excised: there simply is no way back from that imaginary page to the social inscriptions exacted upon it. The temptations of pouring the sheer materiality of architecture's realization as building through the sieve of a liquefying linguistic discourse is nearly irresistible, involving as it does the transformation of structure into magical figurations on a formalist page. This permits sidestepping

Hegemony, in its most complete form, is defined as occurring when the intellectual, moral, and philosophical leadership provided by the class or alliance of classes and class fractions which is ruling, successfully achieves its objective of providing the fundamental outlook for the whole society.[10]

The space of hegemony is not merely that of a localized 'unthought': it is rather a space in which bursts forth a whole conception of the social based upon an intelligibility which reduces its distinct moments to the interiority of a closed paradigm. . . . To construct the concept of hegemony therefore involves not a simply speculative effort within a coherent context, but a more complex strategic movement requiring negotiation among mutually contradictory discursive surfaces. . . . The concept of hegemony supposes a theoretical field dominated by the category of *articulation*; and hence that the articulated elements can be separately identified. . . . In any case, if articulation is a practice, and not the name of a *given* relational complex, it must imply some form of separate presence of the elements which that practice articulates or recomposes.[11]

j.

altogether the socially determinate, the conflictual, the material in favor of the allegories of writing traced into architecture's form.

Jameson has metaphorically been left riding those vertiginous elevators in the Bonaventure Hotel during this critical excursus, and returning to that postmodern theoretical nexus will link the detour to what is distinctive in the practice of Scogin Elam and Bray. Jameson's take on the buildings of postmodernity does not stem from a thoroughly rhetorical or deconstructive analysis, as he is at great pains to enjoin the social and to lament the loss of the totality of the social world

12 Fredric Jameson,
    "Postmodernism and Consumer Society"
    in *Postmodernism and its Discontents,*
    ed. Ann Kaplan (New York: Verso, 1988)
    25.

13 Henry James,
    The American Scene
    (Bloomington: Indiana University
    Press, 1968), 105–6.
    [Originally published in a
    truncated edition in 1907.]

he posits as the precapitalist community. He argues that the fragmentation, illegibility, decentralization, and sheer play of the postmodern are direct results of the hegemony of late capitalism and its accretion in social space in the form of these untoward if magnificent buildings. Jameson insists on the historicity of this process and on the cultural logic with which he identifies it but also turns postmodernism into a lament for the vanished master-narratives. Architecture becomes particularly poignant because it crystallizes the perspectival changes concomitant with this shift in the cultural logic, since Jameson does not see social space as mutable and multiple, in Laclau and Mouffe's terms, but as pervaded with and by the postmodern, a monolithic development best seen in the monuments of architecture. As Jameson puts it:

> This latest mutation in space—postmodern hyperspace—has finally succeeded in transcending the capacities of the individual human body to locate itself, to organize its immediate surroundings perceptually, and cognitively to map its position in a mappable external world. . . . This alarming disjunction point . . . can itself stand as the symbol and analog of that even sharper dilemma which is the incapacity of our minds, at least at present, to map the great global multinational and decentered communicational network in which we find ourselves caught as individual subjects.[12]

Jameson is surely correct about the latter inability to generate this larger conceptual map, but insofar as the hotel stands for the disjunction point of postmodernity, architecture is abstracted from any social network and allegorized as pure psychic form. Architecture is the emblem of social space here much more than other art forms or artifacts can be because social space slips into the space occupied by and transfigured by architectural form.

A critical precursor for Jameson, ironically enough, is Henry James who, in *The American Scene,* is equally, and obsessively, preoccupied with the Waldorf-Astoria Hotel.

> For that is how the place speaks, as great constructed and achieved harmonies mostly speak—as a temple builded, with clustering chapels and shrines, to an idea . . . . Here was a world whose relation to its form and medium was practically imperturbable; here was a conception of publicity *as* the vital medium organized with the authority with which the American genius for organization, put on its mettle alone could organize it. The whole thing remains for me, however, I repeat, a gorgeous, golden blur, a paradise peopled with unmistakable American shapes, yet in which, the general and the particular, the organized and the extemporized, the element of ingenuous joy below and of consummate management above, melted together and left one uncertain which one of them was, at a given turn of the maze, most admiring. . . . There are a thousand forms of this ubiquitous American force, the most ubiquitous of all, that I was in no position to measure; but there was often no resisting a vivid view of the form it may take, on occasion, under pressure of the native conception of the hotel.[13]

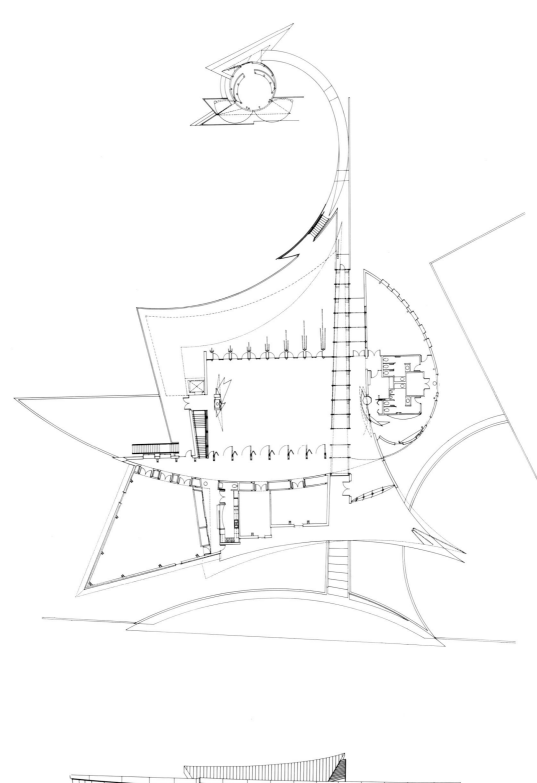

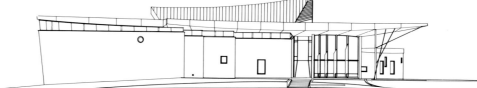

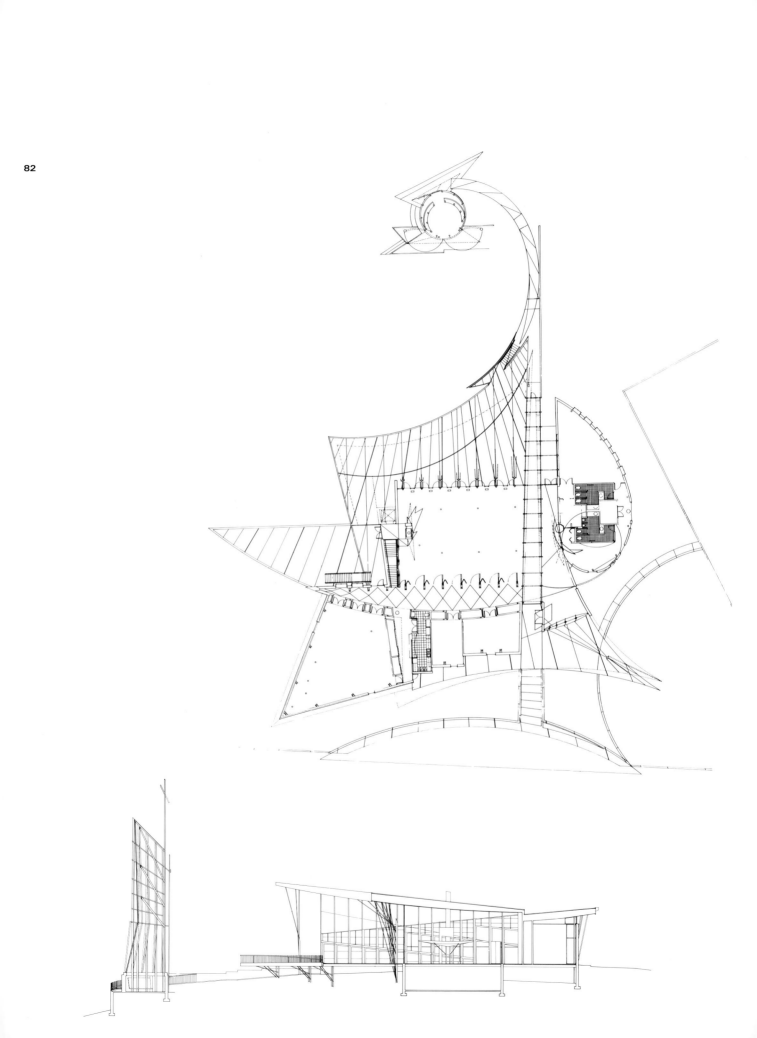

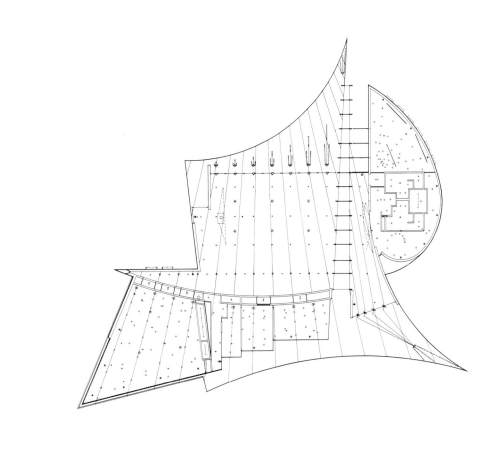

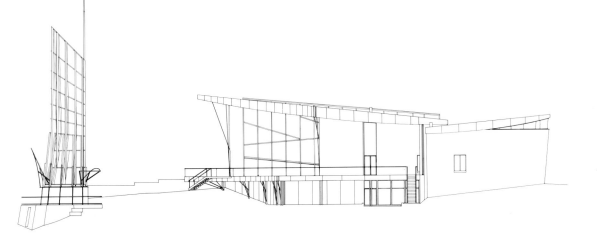

14 William James,
Pragmatism
(Indianapolis:
Hackett, 1981),
29.

James, like Jameson, also sees social space concretized in a building, along perspectival lines, the baffling ones of the commodity culture organizing itself as a labyrinth of reflections, rearranging the social space as a hall of commodifying mirrors. Jameson repeats this experience in his tour of the American scene under the sign of the postmodern, as the reflections of liquidified capital carom off the mirroring glass of the Bonaventure. That dazzle invokes melancholy in both James and Jameson, a delicious melancholy that feeds on the allegory of America it produces. James is dismayed by the publicity he sees writ large in the American building, building as a form of publicity, as a materialization of advertising in gilt and mirrors; Jameson too wanders desolate but secretly euphoric through the maze of corridors, stunned by how late capitalism is able to monumentalize itself through a transformation of social space. The social magic inheres in the circumstance that this sublime effect is brought about by a building, a building looked at not as the artifact of an individual architect's intentionality but as the very carapace of a social structure: an ideology writing itself. There is nothing outside the space of that hotel during the perambulation of either writer because the hotel *is* the consummate social space, needing no other gloss, a crystallization of social relations embodied in architecture [k.]. It is only in the context of rationalized and totally organized public space, like that of the great urban hotel, that interior and very private senses of time and space can properly flourish. Both James and Jameson react to the new senses

of relativism and perspectivism invented and applied to the production of space and the ordering of time, James prophesying on the cusp of modernism, Jameson proposing a glimpse of the postmodern. The two hotels are space-warps, skins of social space that wrap time up and channel, extrude, regulate, or even dizzy it, reflecting social time off the mirrors of social space.

As the geographer David Harvey has pointed out, postmodernity offers another fierce round in the spatialization of

In 1906 William James, Henry's older brother, wrote: "All these you see are *anti-intellectualist* tendencies. Against rationalism as a pretension and a method pragmatism is fully armed and militant. . . . It has no dogmas, and no doctrines save its method. . . . It lies in the midst of our theories, like a corridor in a hotel. Innumerable chambers open out of it. In one you may find a man writing an atheistic volume; in the next some one on his knees praying for strength and faith; in a third a chemist investigating a body's properties. In a fourth a system of idealist metaphysics is being excogitated; in a fifth the impossibility of metaphysics is being shown. But they all own the corridor, and all must pass through it if they want a practicable way of getting into and out of their respective rooms."[14]

k.

15 David Harvey,
"The Rise of Modernism"
in *The Condition of Postmodernity*
(London: Basil Blackwell, 1989),
294.

16 Harvey,
"The Rise of Modernism,"
295–96.

17 Ibid.,
273.

18 Kenneth Frampton,
"Towards a Critical Regionalism"
in *The Anti-Aesthetic*,
ed. Hal Foster (Port Townsend,
Wash.: Bay Press, 1983),
16–30.

88

time that has accelerated throughout the modern period. So acute are the ravages of space-time compression that the home is forced to become a refuge from their exactions and the world's spaces are collapsed into images for viewing on the home screen. Diminishing spatial barriers are part of the logic of flexible accumulation, and geographic mobility and decentralization are important advantages for capital. "As spatial barriers diminish so we become much more sensitized to what the world's spaces contain,"[15] Harvey says, and "The less important the spatial barriers, the greater the sensitivity of capital to the variations of place within space, and the greater the incentive for places to be differentiated in ways attractive to capital."[16] The mobility of this picture takes us back to James and Jameson as they chart the circulation of capital in its highly rarefied traversals of building spaces and perspectives and to the levels of movement suggested by such spatializations. Here the internal contradictions of a deconstructionist postmodernism emerge, becoming particularly acute as space itself is negotiated, traveling from regionalism to internationalism to globalism. Architectural criticism needs a theoretical envoy into those transformations of space and the social relations transpiring out across it. Moreover, such spaces and such traversals are concrete and material and cannot be finessed as intertextuality or the mobility of language on the page.

Postmodernism privileges heterogeneity and difference as liberating forces in the redefinition of cultural discourse. That tendency also gives permission to the fragmentary, partial community articulated in a variety of ways by the catchphrases of several recent theorists: "Lyotard's 'local determinisms,' Stanley Fish's 'interpretive communities,' Michel Foucault's 'heterotopias,' and Kenneth Frampton's 'regional resistances.' Multiple possibilities within which a spatialized 'otherness' can flourish are proposed."[17] Frampton develops this notion with special reference to an architecture of opposition, for example, where only the local can stand against the routine-oriented pressures of corporate building.[18] Lyotard is only able to generate these active speech communities by denying any larger linkages entirely; groups pulsate in a Brownian motion of surprisingly nonconflicting relation. The strictures of global capital that make for unequal access are embarrassments of the meta-narratives that Lyotard eschews. The local can only exist here at the expense or repression of the global. Lyotard in fact goes so far as to say that the world is divided in half—"our" half has as its task to "infinitely complexify," while the other half "must simply survive." This exhortation effectively severs the one task from the other or mystifies the conditions imposing these mutual tasks past the point of recognition. Fish takes up this gauntlet somewhat more prosaically in declaring his willingness simply to accept the fissuring of the social into tiny groups that independently determine their own values and to celebrate those micro-communities in a happy version of pluralism run amok, ignoring the interlocking and conflicting

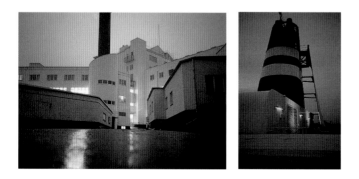

19 See Stanley Fish,
Is There a Text in this Class?
(Cambridge, Mass.: Harvard
University Press, 1985).

20 See Alan Colquhoun,
"Postmodernism and Structuralism:
A Retrospective Glance,"
Assemblage 5 (February 1988):
7–15.

21 Henry-Russell Hitchcock
and Philip Johnson,
The International Style,
(New York: Norton, 1966),
95.

power relations complicating the formation of these interpretive communities and the hierarchies that split and score them.[19]

Architecture's fraught relation with internationalism has long been discussed, especially since it is the focus of architectural modernism, with regionalism serving, as the counter-force, the swerve away from the monolithic, the universalizing, the totalizing. The shapes of internationalism, visionary in their moment or at least capable of a utopian political cast, are discredited in theory, at least [l.]. What replaces that internationalism, at the level of theory, however? Critical regionalism has at its heart the laudable goal of defining a critical architecture, a premise for returning contemporary architecture to its social engagements, but there are some problems. For one, regionalism is locked in a death dance with its spurned partner internationalism, so frozen in repudiation of this mode that all of its gestures merely replicate the flip side of its "other." Such a regionalism also fantasizes a local conversation, a regional "essence" that, however desirable in utopian terms, cannot be located anywhere on the map of postmodern reality. The preservationist and idiomatic references that have arisen out of critical regionalism are all to the good, but a complete regionalist program founders on the politics of the global, which cannot be waved away by the magic wand of a regionally sensitive architecture. The social space, after all, is at least as much constituted by the informational, representational networks of mass culture and media as by anything else, and a regional purism will throw out the baby of social reality with the bath water of internationalism. [20]

One could retort that critical regionalism fosters an architectural exit from the nets of the mass culture, seen as a passive, enslaving, commoditized culture industry menacing on all inherent regional qualities. And indeed, this is true where franchise chains push aside regional styles and forms. I propose that such an attitude toward mass culture is intensely problematic, suggesting as it does that the consuming that mass culture implies is simply mindless ideological incorporation, in which deadly cultural menaces are painlessly absorbed into the bloodstream. A stance between

The international style is broad and elastic enough for many varying talents and for many decades of development. . . . Those who have buried architecture, whether from a thwarted desire to continue the past or from an over-anxiety to modify and hurry on the future, have been premature: We have an architecture still. [21]

l.

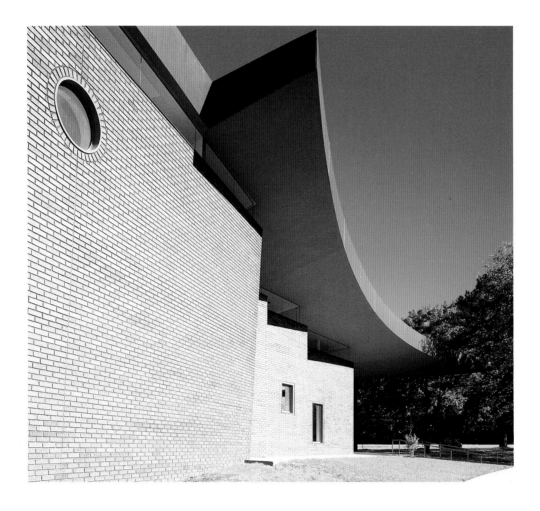

22 Michel de Certeau,
The Practice of Everyday Life
(Berkeley: University of California Press, 1984);
idem, *Heterologies: Discourse on the Other*
(Minneapolis: University of Minnesota, 1985).

23 Pierre Bordieu,
*Distinction: A Social Critique
of the Judgement of Taste*
(Cambridge, Mass.: Harvard
University Press, 1984).

these two needs to be explored where consumption can also be read as a productive labor, received mass cultural forms then entering into a complex, productive, and unpredictable set of meanings and strategies. Both Michel de Certeau and Pierre Bourdieu have offered correctives to the vision of mass culture's static and viselike grip, de Certeau by examining the tactical uses of power in everyday life by those who appropriate mass culture for their own purposes (what in *The Practice of Everyday Life* he calls the "tactics" of the subjects of mass culture[22]) and Bourdieu by expanding our notion of the social field to encompass the labor performed in receiving and recirculating mass cultural forms.[23]

These questions really do impinge on architecture when what one wants is to theorize a globalism—an understanding of the urban in the conditions of modern life, a global phenomenon in its ramifications—that doesn't deny the material reality of social experience, that acknowledges the interconnections between places under the (uncomfortable) sign of corporate capital, that doesn't seek to efface or evade the multiple differences which obtain among regions, communities, countries, and first, second, and third worlds (if these latter distinctions can even be made) but that can theorize social space as dialectically open. This implies going beyond a concentration on the local trope of the building, however aesthetically important, and beyond the figurations and defigurations of a seductive linguistic paradigm or a notion of an endless "free play," to look *also* at the accretions of social power and social memory, a history not of quotations or virtually textual references but a made, material history. A reading of Scogin Elam and Bray would necessarily rest on such critical possibilities. The building as singular emblem, however extravagantly textualized, however intricately inscripted, can never take us in that direction.

A second, more literal excursus into social space now follows, in the form of a concrete experience of the architecture to set in motion, with those of James and Jameson, an excursion of sorts that, despite its specificity, might also typify an encounter with postmodern "building." Those who came to Atlanta, some for the first time, to participate in the conference "Critical Architecture/ Architectural Criticism" were, within an hour of arrival, whisked into a small van for a tactical sweep of the city, a city now coded as a constellation of the individually pulsating star-sites of its architectural constructions. That aleatory grid was thrown like a net over an urban space rendered unfamiliar even to its residents, so much so that the main landmarks of recognition were these sites, which I had pored over in slides and drawings many times before [m.]. Rather than landing, as did Jameson, within the precincts of one overpowering hotel, a fantasmagoria of the postmodern writ as a singular building, the architectural pilgrims were taken on a surgical incursion through the city along the Ariadne's thread of Scogin Elam and Bray, with the nodal points or knots varying from the svelte interiors of the Herman Miller Showroom to the tensile shapes

PLATTUS *The real life of
our tour yesterday was Jeff's
running commentary on the
culture of Atlanta and traces
of his past life. Without that
I think the whole experience
would have been a lot flatter
and the map that is drawn
of the city, that Jennifer
talked about, by individual
buildings, would have been
a lot more pallid.*

m.

24 Edward Said,
"Traveling Theory,"
The World, the Text and the Critic
(Cambridge, Mass.: Harvard
University Press, 1983).

of the Buckhead Library, the spill of wood and play of shadow at the High Museum at Georgia Pacific Center, and the extraordinary Candler School of Theology (still having last-minute punch-list work done), to the more private meditative space of the Chmar House, set like a ship in the woods. The tour took place in the encapsulating bubble of the van rather than in the scopic space of the glass-enclosed elevator—the traversal was horizontal instead of vertical, not only in the literal sense but in the mobility or motility of its penetration of urban space. Jameson's discussion evaporates the city by infusing it into the building itself, and while Jameson is right that Portman's hotel insinuates a city within itself, the failure to consider the dialectic between that simulacral city and its urban setting allegorizes the building as a kind of freestanding, freeze-dried shard of eviscerated social space.

In contrast, our rather madcap trip through the city of Atlanta, filtered through the mode of pilgrimage to sacred sites but shot through with the contradictions of billboards, traffic, and reminiscences, was about architecture as a practice—not architecture as excrescence, however beautiful [n.]. The sites are mutually informing, because they exist in dialogy, to use Bakhtin's term, with the city surround and in a palimpsestic relation to one another—the curvilinear walls, the punctured soaring spaces of light, the idiom of the round window, the arch mythography explored at each place. The experience of viewing these buildings was particular to the conference and its focus, but the manner in which these buildings allow themselves to be apprehended is a corrective to a monolithic, an apocalyptic, or an agency-free characterization of the postmodern urban space. These artifacts are not related to their sites in either the nullifying bravura style of the Bonaventure or in any facile straining after a vernacular idiom or "translation" of a presumed populism; in addition they don't operate as self-consuming artifacts or exercises in figural undoing. Each building addresses the circumstances—social, aesthetic, and commercial—of its being viewed in this place, for this reason. Such architecture doesn't turn its back on the regional but infuses it with a witty and incisive representation of the "outside;" such an architecture doesn't gesture toward totalization, even of the visual field, but offers a play of formal *and* social referents, an intellectual challenge to the puzzles of social space that has none of the portentousness of the shepherding architectural mentality visible in, for example, the work of Michael Graves or Charles Moore. These buildings *could* be moved, could travel, but they insouciantly appear at this moment to choose not to be relocated. Edward Said has introduced the evocative phrase "traveling theory" into our critical lexicons, in an eponymous article.[24] His concern in this influential essay was with how well theory could indeed travel, how readily it could be pried apart from its chosen models for analysis and its habitual sites of interpretation to go on the open road of a larger, indeed more global, scene of mobile theorization. Such travel demands the ability to travel light—not theoretically

unequipped but with versatile and ingenious critical tools. This versatility and nomadic spirit appears in the critical architectural baggage of Scogin Elam and Bray. Working locally, they think globally, in that all of the projects are lovingly site-specific but also dense with other referents, aware of the relations subtending the sites. To accomplish this, it would seem, their practice devotes equal attention to the "imaginary" structure, the fantasmatic and private associations of the building on paper, and to the material relations of its actual unfolding, of how it will be seen and used and indeed felt and remembered within social space. Their work has the liminal quality of travel between these mediums, where the textual or figural or semiotic is not privileged beyond the relational, the dialogic, the spatial. The resulting building doesn't stand as an allegory of forces inherent in building as such, nor do their buildings serve as allegories, even allegorical ruins, of their own theorization. Scogin Elam and Bray's work avoids the implosion of the self-referential in favor of the invigorating and expansive openings into social space that their buildings demarcate. No building dominates its site or demands a mental excision of itself from its surroundings; these buildings instead resonate where they are as well as point beyond themselves, with what can only be called the wit and the confidence of traveling light.

25 Jeffrey Kipnis,
    In the Manor of Nietzsche:
    Aphorisms Around and About Architecture,
    (New York: Calluna Farms Press, 1990),
    n.p.

Literary and cultural theorists as well as architectural critics can ponder this work as highly instructive for those attempting to bridge theory and practice, in search of theory that is at once semiotic or linguistic and entirely material and social. The ability to understand a *practice* or to see it represented, as in Scogin Elam and Bray's collective work, as a practice building rather than a building which is held to stand for all practice, is the very direction theory must travel as it goes global. Their work is *overdetermined* (a word with little currency in deconstructive thought but integral to any fusing of theory and practice): overdeterminate in allowing the play of difference and the decentering of subjectivity to elide with the historically contradictory and the social as a contested space [o.].

A building like the Candler School of Theology doesn't implode with the excess baggage of textual allegory; it is thoroughly alert to the reading of its surfaces but puts a spin on those in refusing the triumphal isolation of "textuality" or the self-aggrandizing rhetoric of the emblematic building. Scogin Elam and Bray make you think on-site; their buildings prompt thinking as a site-specific activity, although directed outward to larger webs of relation and connection. This thinking is neither the psychic paralysis nor the "schizophrenia" of Jameson's postmodernity, and especially not the laborious and even coy connoisseur-thought implied by many self-defined "postmodern" buildings: their exhilarating site-specific thought casts a net over regional images and memories, international styles and urban devices, and a wider contemplation of the place of the contemporary building today, and such thought doesn't merely read off a textual page, however intricate, or pose the building as a textual conundrum. Its practice is more at ease, more various, and more dynamic. Where a certain line of current architectural theory still valorizes the "disintegrations" of ordered form or privileges the allegory of the singular building (in textual ruins), Scogin Elam and Bray go beyond these readings. Their disarticulations of formal, architectural space at the same time rearticulate a social, shared discourse. In that sense, their work succeeds in building a practice, a practice of critical thought and critical architecture, a practice of building on social space.

Deconstruction in three easy lessons:

a) The meaning of any work is undecidable.
b) In as much as they aspire to the
   meaningful, conventional ways of
   working, whether radical or conservative,
   always seek to repress undecidability.
c) It is both possible and desirable to work
   in such a way to respect undecidability,
   that is, to produce a work which is
   neither meaningful nor meaningless. [25]

o.

Artemisia, Aristotle, and the View from L.A.

Ann Bergren

1 Aristotle and Mausolus, London, British Museum. See C. Mitchell, *Hellenistic Art* (Greenwich, Conn.: New York Graphic Society, n.d.) fig.18.

2 See Kenneth Frampton, "Towards a Critical Regionalism: Six Points for an Architecture of Resistance" in *The Anti-Aesthetic: Essays on Postmodern Culture,* ed. Hal Foster (Port Townsend, Wash.: Bay Press, 1983), 16–30.

In some places in the South, for a short period in warm weather in the woods after dark, an architecture of sound and light emerges. A reverse meteor shower; the lightning bugs rise from the grasses making a blinking, deep fabric of darkness and fluorescent sequins. The tree frog symphony fills in all the spaces of darkness between the blinks.

Merrill Elam

I raced motorcycles, now I race architecture.

Mack Scogin to Merrill Elam

THE COUPLING OF THE CRITICAL GAZE

The English word critical derives from the Greek verb **krino** *to discern, separate, distinguish.*

When I look at the work of Scogin Elam and Bray, I gaze through this window photographed by Merrill Elam and shown in her lecture at SCI-Arc in the fall of 1989—a lecture whose visions are never absent from this paper. "You look at my window from the outside and I look at it from the inside."

What do I, a professor of Classics and architectural theory living in Los Angeles, discern, when I look at the work of Scogin Elam and Bray? I discern the couple Artemisia and Aristotle as they are coupled through my view of the Classics from L.A. [a.][1].

I see this Classical couple with a "female" gaze [b.]. The male and female gaze are constructions.

They are constructed with relevance for what has been known as critical architecture and architecture criticism, upon the experience of seeing one's *sexe*—not "critical regionalism"[2] but what we might call "regional criticism," discernment of the region of one's body.

A male can see his own. He can see

I adopt the concept of the "gaze" from Jacques Lacan, "Of the Gaze as *Object Petit a,*" *The Four Fundamental Concepts of Psycho-Analysis,* trans. Alan Sheridan (New York: W.W. Norton, 1978), 67–119. The gaze is the visual counterpart of language. Together these modes constitute the subject, as "said" and "seen" respectively. Lacan does not distinguish between a male and a female gaze. Like language, the gaze belongs to the symbolic mode of the phallus and the "name of the father." From the Lacanian perspective, there could no more be a "female gaze" than a "female language," the female's distinctive *jouissance* being beyond discourse and knowledge. Properly speaking, there is no female substantive and any definite article used with a female should be overmarked with a slash sign /. See Lacan, "God and the *Jouissance* of Woman," trans. Jacqueline Rose in *Feminine Sexuality. Jacques Lacan and the école freudienne,* ed. Juliet Mitchell and Jacqueline Rose (New York and London: W.W. Norton, 1982), 137–148. Recognizing the psychoanalytic account of the role of the sight of the female genitals in the construction of gender, I construct the distinction between the male and female gaze by analogy with the difference between the reaction of the male and the female to the sight of the **anasyrma** "raising of the skirt." In the Greek mythology of Baubo, sight of her exposed genitals evokes laughter from the mourning goddess Demeter and the return of fertility in women and the earth. When it is the object of the "male gaze," such exposure produces fear and flight. Freud refers to the Baubo myth and its apparent representation in the terracotta figurines from Priene (see [c.]) in his 1916 paper, "A Mythological Parallel to a Visual Obsession" (*SE* XIV.337–338) and analyzes the male response to such visions in "Medusa's Head" (*SE* X.105–106): "what arouses horror in oneself will produce the same effect upon the enemy against whom one is seeking to defend oneself. We read in Rabelais of how the Devil took to flight when the woman showed him her vulva." See also Ann Bergren, "Baubo and Helen. Gender in the Irreparable Wound," *Drawing, Building, Text. Essays in Architectural Theory and Criticism,* ed. Andrea Kahn (New York: Princeton Architectural Press, 1991), 107–126.

b.

a.

[3] Baubo, Fourth-century B.C. terracotta found in the sanctuary of Demeter at Priene, Antiquarium, Berlin. See *Before Sexuality*, ed. David Halperin, et al. (Princeton: Princeton University Press, 1990), 110, fig. 3.1.

[4] The Caryatids of the Erecthrum on the Acropolis.

[5] See Ann Bergren, "Helen's 'Good Drug': Odyssey IV 1–305," *Contemporary Literary Hermeneutics and the Interpretation of Classical Texts*, ed. Stephen Kresic (Ottawa: University of Ottawa Press, 1981), 200–14.

[6] See Ann Bergren, "Language and the Female in Early Greek Thought," *Arethusa* "Semiotics and Classical Studies" 6.1–2 (1983): 69–95.

[7] Watts Towers, Simon Rodia.

[8] See, for example, *Metaphysics* Book I, 1.1–3.2.

its presence or its absence by looking at himself. He can discern, separate, distinguish between the presence of his sex and its absence and whether it is high or low. A male can see (his sex directly) and discern (its) "hierarchy." This is a gaze of replacement. A female cannot see her own [c.][3]. She can see her *sexe* only in the mirror, only by looking at another (like her) self. This is a gaze of reflection and refraction [d.][4].

The discernment, the separation, the distinction—the "criticism"—of these two gazes is by its construction not fixed. It is subject to a kind of inebriation, resulting in what may be called the "gaze of Helen."[5] To gaze (as male) at Helen and to gaze as Helen is to divide the object (the bodily region) into oscillating doubles, a relation of the **tropos** *turning* in which one double turns into the other. When the Greek poet Stesichorus said that men died for Helen at Troy, he suffered blindness: a figure of castration, the condition of having no sex—neither male nor female—to be criticized one way or the other. To get back his sight and his *sexe*, Stesichorus composed a **palinôidia** *palinode, recantation* saying that the "true" Helen went to Egypt, while only her **eidolon** *image* went to Troy. To gaze (as male) at Helen, Stesichorus had to discern, separate, distinguish two Helens, the true and the **eidolon**. But who can tell the two apart? For the death of the men at Troy for the image was all too true.[6]

My view from L.A. turns into the "gaze of Helen" as I trace the couple Aristotle and Artemisia [e.]. In the architecture and in the critical context of the architecture of Scogin Elam and Bray—in the "South," as one might say, looking in the window from the outside. There I see an oscillating, tropic coupling of the gaze of Aristotle and the gaze of Artemisia, the aristocracy of Aristotle and the **mêtis** of Artemisia, the hierarchy of Aristotle and the polytropy of Artemisia —a couple joined under the sign of the "folly" [f.][7].

BERGREN *Mack, what do you think is the value of an event such as this?*

SCOGIN *The selfish value is that we're interested in evolving our architecture, and without critical statements from outside it's impossible.*

BERGREN *Does this event really contribute to the development of a practice?*

SCOGIN *This meeting today? We're talking about our practice, and it's all getting to be rather personal. I would prefer to talk about it on a broader scope. In Atlanta we're making the city, you can really feel it. And we're making it without critical judgment. That's almost to the point of absurdity. There is not a value present to gauge against, to challenge against. You end up developing your own set of values (which may not be all that bad, frankly), but when it's not put within the context of scholarly and knowledgeable critical judgment from the outside, I think it lacks a certain substance, which makes it difficult for people like ourselves to continue to critically evolve.*

THE GAZE OF ARISTOTLE

The gaze of Aristotle is made up of elements from his texts.

From Aristotle's *Metaphysics* comes the "view"—as we say, following Aristotle—that sight is knowledge or knowledge is visual.[8] This "view" of knowledge as visual assumes a stable distinction between the presence and absence of the thing seen: you can know it—in Greek, you "have seen it"—only if what you see is really there to the exclusion of everything else [g.]. This is a gaze of replacement.

From Aristotle's *Nichomachean Ethics* comes the view that

In Greek, the verb "to know" is the perfect tense of the verb "to see:" **oida** *I have seen, I know*.

e.   d.   f.   c.   g.

[9] See, for example, *Politics* Book 1, 1–2.

[10] See *Poetics*, chapters 1–13. See also Northrup Frye, *Anatomy of Criticism* (Princeton: Princeton University Press, 1957), 33–35.

the political philosopher is an architect: that the architect builds literally what the philosopher as figurative architect designs [h.].

From the *Politics* comes that political design: the design of aristocracy as slavery.[9] It is the founding formulation in Western culture of social, racial, and sexual hierarchy, the architectural "positing" of a "natural" inferiority of race and gender that justifies both slavery and the "rule of the father" in marriage and the family.

From the *Poetics* comes a doctrine of genre and critical value that depends upon "mimetic level." This doctrine inadvertently "deconstructs" the foundation of the *Politics'* "natural" hierarchies. In the *Poetics* Aristotle says that any **poiêsis** *making* is a **mimêsis** *imitation* and that genre—whether something is a tragedy or a comedy, for example—depends upon the level of the thing imitated vis-à-vis "ourselves"[10] (as Aristotle puts it, assuming, as he does, that all of "ourselves" are Athenian citizens, that is to say, males, since females cannot be citizens in Athens). The tragic hero is of a higher "mimetic level" than we in all respects except his **hamartia** *missing of the mark*, while the comic hero is lower—a slave, a woman, a sausagemaker. The mimetic level of tragedy is thus relatively high. Epic, too, is "high mimetic" because its heroes are often half divine. Sacred text or myth is thus of the "highest mimetic level" because it imitates gods, while representation of those at the same level as "ourselves" produces "middle mimetic" realism and of those below us, "low mimetic" comedy and irony.

Although appearing to be absolute, this theory of genre is in fact relative and thereby inadvertently revolutionary, inadvertently deconstructive of the natural hierarchy of value that it stipulates. For this definition of the genre depends not upon the intrinsic status or value of the object, but upon the value perceived or assigned by the observer. If you are a god attending the *Oedipus Rex*, the drama is not a tragedy, because the character imitated is "below" you. If you are a relative of one of the Suitors of Penelope, the *Odyssey* is not a **kleos** *epic praise poetry* but a **threnos** *dirge*. In deconstructing natural hierarchy, the Aristotelian theory of genre as "mimetic level" thus does not get rid of hierarchical relations—deconstruction is not destruction—it does not get rid of values and statuses. It rather tropes them: it puts them in a relation of the **tropos** *turning*.

It is this potential for trope within the Aristotelian gaze that makes it available for coupling with the gaze of Artemisia.

THE GAZE OF ARTEMISIA

The gaze of Artemisia reflects her building. Her construction is a non-Platonic paradigm of an architectural power heretofore repressed, but forever buttressing Classical philosophy and philo-

See, e.g., *Nichomachean Ethics* Book 7.11. While appropriating the constructive power of the architect, Aristotle's terminology elevates the political philosopher above his namesake. For, since the **polis** *city-state* is the sole commissioner of major works until the Hellenistic period, it is the designs of political power that the architect builds. In keeping with the superiority of mind (identified with the male) over material (identified with the female) throughout Aristotelian philosophy, but in contrast with the regular superiority of the literal model over metaphorical copy throughout Greek philosophy, Aristotle's terminology creates a hierarchy in which the literal architect builds in matter the figurative architect's formal constructions. By a similar strategy, Platonic philosophy adopts the architectural art for its divine exemplar, the demiurge of the *Timaeus*, while relegating the human **demiourgos** in the *Laws* to the status of a virtual female, deprived of citizenship. See Ann Bergren, "Architecture Gender Philosophy," *Strategies in Architectural Thinking*, ed. Richard Burdett, Jeffrey Kipnis, and John Whiteman (Cambridge, Mass.: Chicago Institute for Architecture and Urbanism/MIT Press, forthcoming 1992).

h.

11 See Simon Hornblower, *Mausolus* (Oxford: Oxford University Press, 1982) on Artemisia and Mausolus.

12 See Karl Jeppersen, *The Mausoleion at Halikarnassos. Reports of the Danish Archaeological Expedition to Bodrum* vol. 2, *The Written Sources* Jutland Archaeological Society Publications 15.2 (Copenhagen: Aarhus University Press, 1986) on the Mausoleum and Artemisia's building.

sophical architecture. It is the power of **mêtis**, the *transformative intelligence* common to every **technê** [i.].

Artemisia was a builder. She was part of a building couple. She and Mausolus, her husband and brother, planned the construction of his tomb, the Mausoleum [j.]. After his death she built it.[11] It was praised as one of the Seven Wonders of the World. She also built a memorial to her own constructions. It was walled over and declared an

> **abaton: a + baton** (< **baino** *to step*) *not + stepped upon*,
> hence *impassible* (mountains), *unfordable* (rivers),
> *inaccessible, desolate, not to be stepped upon, pure* (holy places),
> *not ridden* (horses, female animals)
> = **adyton** *innermost sanctuary, shrine.*

In *De Architectura* II.8.13-16 "On Walling" Vitruvius describes the walls and city of Halicarnassus as built by King Mausolus, brother and husband of Artemisia [k.][12]. From the royal palace, the king could see to the right—the forum, harbor, and whole circuit of walls, and to the left—a secret harbor lying hidden under the mountains, so that no one could see what was going on in it.

Vitruvius then tells the story of how Artemisia used the harbor in the course of her own construction [l.].

When, after the death of Mausolus, his wife Artemisia began to reign, the Rhodians considered it unbecoming, shameful, intolerable, and harsh [**indignantes**] that a woman should rule over the cities throughout Caria. So they armed a fleet and set out to invade and occupy that kingdom.

When this was reported to Artemisia, she ordered the fleet to be hidden in that harbor, equipped with concealed rowers and marines, and the rest of the citizens to be in the wall [**in muro esse**].

But when the Rhodians had landed with their fleet splendidly equipped [**ornata**], she ordered all the citizens to give them applause from the wall [**ab muro**] and to promise that they would hand over the town.

When the Rhodians had penetrated within the wall [**intra murum**] with their ships left behind empty, Artemisia suddenly—

Compare Vernant and Detienne, 296 ff. for the **mêtis** of navy stratagems as directly inspired by the techniques of fishing. For the Artemisia of the Battle of Marathon (ancestress of the wife and sister of Mausolus) as their exemplar, see Herodotus, *Persian Wars* Book 8, 87ff.

On the tomb in the Hegelian theory of architecture, see, e.g., Georg W.F. Hegel, *Aesthetics. Lectures on Fine Art*, trans. Thomas Knox (Oxford: Oxford University Press, 1975), vol. 2, 630–700, esp. 650–54 on the pyramids and the mausoleum, the latter demonstrating "the special purpose of architecture, namely to furnish an enclosure merely." See also Daniel Payot, *Le philosophe et l'architecte* (Paris: Aubier Montaigne, 1982), 29-50; and Jacques Derrida, "The Pit and the Pyramid: Introduction to Hegel's Semiology,"*Margins of Philosophy*, trans. Alan Bass (Chicago: University of Chicago Press, 1982), 69–108, first published in *Marges de la philosophie* (Paris: Minuit, 1972), 79–127.

The essential work on **mêtis** is by Marcel Detienne and Jean-Pierre Vernant, *Cunning Intelligence in Greek Culture and Society,* trans. Janet Lloyd (Atlantic Highlands, N.J.: The Harvester Press, 1978), first published as *Les ruses d'intelligence: la Mêtis des grecs.* (Paris: Flammarion, 1974). For the work and the intelligence of the artisan as **mêtis**, see Perre Vidal-Naquet, "A Study in Ambiguity: Artisans in the Platonic City" in *The Black Hunter: Forms of Thought and Forms of Society in the Greek World*, trans. Andrew Szegedy-Maszac (Baltimore: The Johns Hopkins University Press, 1986), 224–45, first published as "Étude d'une ambiguïté: les artisans dans la cité platonicienne," *Le chasseur noir. Formes de pensée et formes de société dans le monde grec* (Paris: Maspero, 1981), 289–316, esp. 227–28. For the architect as a master of **mêtis**, see Zoe Petrie, "Trophonius ou l'architecte. À propos du statut des techniciens dans la cité grecque," *Studii Clasice.* 18 (1979): 23–37.

k.   l.   j.   i.

13 See George Hersey,
The Lost Meaning of Classical Architecture
(Cambridge, Mass.: MIT Press 1988),
esp. 1–10 and 69–75 on the trophy and
the trope (< Greek *tropos* 'turning')
in the formation of classical architecture.

14 See, e.g.,
Symposium 211a,
for the Form as unitiary
and unchanging.

106

through a trench she had made into the sea—led her fleet out from that smaller harbor and thus sailed into the greater one. The Rhodians had no place to retreat. Closed up [*conclusi*] in the middle, they were butchered in the forum itself.

Then Artemisia put her own rowers and soldiers in the Rhodians' ships and set out for Rhodes. When the Rhodians saw their own ships coming wreathed with laurel, they thought their citizens were returning victorious and admitted the enemy [m.].

After capturing Rhodes and killing the leading citizens, Artemisia set up a trophy [13] of her victory in the city and made two bronze statues, one of the Rhodian state and the other in her own image. She formed it [*figuravit*] placing the brands of slavery [*stigmata*] on the state of Rhodes.

Afterwards the Rhodians were impeded [*impediti bound at the feet*] by religious scruple—because it is an impiety to dislocate [*removeri move back again*] a trophy, once it has been dedicated. So around that place they constructed a building. And they protected [*texerunt covered*] it by the erection of a Greek guardhouse [*erecta Graia statione*] so that no one could look upon it. And they ordered it to be called [*abaton not to be stepped upon*].

Inside the **abaton** of Artemisia is **mêtis**.

Mêtis is both the working and the work of *transformative intelligence*. **Mêtis** means both the transformative process common to every **technê** and the products of **technê** as well. **Mêtis** embraces mind and hand, language and material. It integrates powers and activities separated in aesthetic traditions that draw a hard line between the verbal and the visual, the linguistic and the plastic, the written text and the building [n.].

Mêtis makes transforming form.

Consequently, there can be no Platonic Form of **mêtis**, as there can be no Form of matter. A Platonic Form is unitary, unchanging, and immobile, forever **homoion** like to itself [14] [o.]. Thus there can be no Form of the multiple, the constantly "other." There can "be" no Being of Proteus. **Mêtis**, in fact, resists the Platonic story of Being. By insisting that the constructive power of mind as well as matter lies in its irreducibly material property of changing form, **mêtis** would aggrandize philosophy with architecture and accord to non-material meaning the power of transformation.

As it can never wholly elude **mêtis**, no building or writing can ever attain the Formal status that the Classical tradition of critical architecture and architectural criticism has claimed for itself. Nonetheless, the semantic field of words and themes associated with **mêtis** composes the analytic vocabulary of a comprehensive and discerning architectural program.

With Artemisia's disguising of her troups, compare the strategy of the Argive poetess Telesilla who drove out the invading Spartans by ordering the women of Argos to take up arms and man the walls, a victory commemorated in a yearly festival called **Hybristika** *The Acts of Hybris* for which women wore men's clothes and men wore women's dresses and veils (see Plutarch, *Moralia*, "On the Bravery of Women" 245) and Odysseus' return home disguised as a beggar to test the loyalty of his household and to defeat the Suitors.

For example, English *draw* vs. *write* (though *draw* means *write* in "draw a contract"), French *dessiner* vs. *écrire*, German *zeichnen* vs. *schreiben*, Italian *disegnare* vs. *scrivere*. On the glossary of drawing see Jacques Derrida, "Cartouches," *The Truth in Painting*, trans. Geoff Bennington and Ian McLeod (Chicago: The University of Chicago Press, 1987), 185–247, esp, 191–93, first published in *La vérité en peinture* (Paris: Flammarion, 1978) 213–89. For painting (**zôgraphia** *writing/drawing living things*) as a special case of writing (**graphé** *writing*), since in both cases the graphic object remains silent when questioned, see Plato, *Phaedrus* 275d4–7.

In Platonic idiom to be *true to yourself* is to be *like* or *same*; see, e.g., *Symposium* 173d4, *Republic* 549e2. For the collocation of *like* and *true* as synonymous, see *Sophist* 252d1 and *Philebus* 65d2–3; as reciprocal, *Phaedrus* 273d1–6. The basis of this relation is the *likeness* or *sameness* of the sensible particular and the intelligible Form or paradigm; see, e.g., *Republic* 472c9–d1, *Parmenides* 132d1–4 (where the participation of the particular in the paradigm is precisely the relation of likeness) and *Sophist* 264c–268d.

m.   n.   o.

BRIDGE AT CONCOURSE

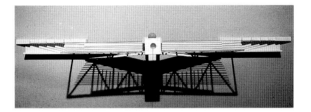

[15] Marcel Detienne and Jean-Pierre Vernant, *Cunning Intelligence in Greek Culture and Society,* trans. Janet Lloyd (Atlantic Highlands, N.J.: The Harvester Press, 1978), 26.

[16] Ibid., 294–95.

[17] Ibid., 305.

[18] Ibid., 37.

[19] Ibid., 46.

SEMANTIC FIELD OF *METIS*

mêtis is

pantoie multiple   *poikile* variegated   *aiole* shifting

"all qualities which betray the polymorphism and polyvalence of a kind of intelligence which, to render itself impossible to seize and to dominate fluid, changing realities, must always prove itself more supple and more polymorphic." [15]

shape-shifting

imitate the enemy (or lure the enemy to imitate you) to beat him at his own game

mêtis is

tropos turning   *polutropie* of many turns

reversal

complicity of putatively formal opposites
the reversal and the circle as polymorphous doubles

circle

in rotation both mobile and immobile, moving in both directions at once [p.].

bond

"the net is a composition of woven or plaited links and its structure marks it out as the epitomy of the bond for it is both bound together and, at the same time, its effect is to bind . . . it is *apeiron*, without limit, and circular." [16]

"Metis cannot be deployed without this fundamental combination of the bond and the circle. To exercise all its powers the intelligence of cunning needs the circular reciprocity between what is bound and what is binding." [17]

joint

plekein knot   *strephein* twist   *sumplekein* interweave

octopus architecture

"a knot made up of a thousand arms, a living, interlacing, network, a *poluplokos* of many twists being . . . the same adjective used to describe the labyrinth, with its mazes and tangle of halls and passages" [18]

[of the octopus and the cuttlefish]

"They have neither front nor rear, they swim sideways with their eyes in front and their mouth behind, their heads haloed by the waving feet. When these creatures mate, they do so mouth to mouth and arm to arm. Thus closely linked, they swim along together: the front of the one is the rear of the other. They are oblique creatures the

The ultimate expression of these qualities is the circle, the bond that is perfect because it completely turns back on itself, is closed in on itself, with neither beginning nor end, front nor rear, and which in rotation becomes both mobile and immobile, moving in both directions at once . . . the circle unites within it several opposites each one giving birth to its opposite, it appears as the strangest, most baffling thing in the world, *thaumasiôtaton*, possessing a power which is beyond ordinary logic. [19]

p.

20 Detienne and
    Vernant, 38.
21 Ibid., 39.
22 Ibid., 48.

23 Homer,
    Iliad Book 10,
    line 19.

24 Homer,
    Iliad Book 7, line 324;
    Book 9, lines 93–95, 422;
    Book 13, lines 303, 386;
    idem, *Odyssey* Book 4, lines 678, 739;
    Hesiod, *Shield of Heracles*, line 28.

25 *Iliad* Book 6,
    line 187;
    Odyssey Book 9,
    line 422.

26 Plato,
    Laws,
    823d–824a.

27 Detienne and
    Vernant, 37.
28 Ibid., 35
    (quoting Oppian,
    Treatise on Hunting, III,
    449–60).

29 Ibid., 33.
30 Ibid., 35–37.

front of which is never distinctly distinguished from the rear, and in their being and in the way they move, they create a confusion of directions."[20]

model of **poluplokon noema** *intelligence of many twists or coils*

characteristic of sophist and politician[21]

mêtis is

mechane *artifice*

"the sleights of hand and trade secrets which give craftsmen their control over material which is always more or less intractable to their designs"[22]

mêtis is

technê *craft, skill*

metal work and carpentry

tektaineto mêtin *build a* **mêtis**[23]   **tektainô** *build* cf. **archi–tecktôn**

weaving

goddess Metis: mother of Athena, who teaches women to weave

weave a **mêtis**[24]   *weave a* **dolos**[25]

movement of reversal: warp and woof

mêtis is

dolos *trick, trap, lure*

hunting and fishing [26] [q.]

mêtis of hunter vs. **mêtis** of hunted

reversal

"fox-fish" turns its body inside out

interior becomes exterior and the hook falls out[27]

imitate defeat

fox reverses itself, plays dead, and turns into a trap for the hunter [r.]

foxy architecture

"'The dwelling that it [the fox] digs itself has seven different entrances linked by as many corridors and the openings are situated a long way from each other. Thus it has less cause to fear that hunters, laying a trap at its door, will make it fall into their snares.'. . . The misleading, enigmatic, polymorphic earth of the fox is matched by the animal's equally impenetrable mind."[28]

When, in the *Laws*, Plato violently condemns line fishing, the hunting of aquatic creatures, the use of weels, the hunting of birds and all forms of hunting with nets and traps, he does so because all these techniques foster the qualities of cunning and duplicity which are diametrically opposed to the virtues that the city of the *Laws* demanded from its citizens. [29]

q.

There is no positive evidence based on observation to corroborate the amazing behavior which so many writers attribute to the fox—be it the actual fox or the fish. It was not in nature that the Greeks found this type of reversal behavior in animals, but rather in their own minds, in the conception that they formed of **mêtis**, its methods and effects. The fox, being the embodiment of cunning, can only behave as befits the nature of an intelligence full of wiles. If it turns back on itself it is because it is, itself, as it were, **mêtis**, the power of reversal. [30]

r.

31 Detienne
and Vernant, 29.

110

lure

"The fleshy appendage growing on the fishing frog is a true fishing bait and as such has a double character: to the little fish it looks for all the world like food but it is food which soon changes itself into a voracious maw. With this type of ligament dangling from its neck which it can stretch out and draw back at will, the fishing frog sets up a manoeuvre which equals the art of line fishing."[31]

32 Ibid., 39. 33 Ibid., 37. 34 Ibid., 30.
(for Eumetis, see Plutarch,
Banquet of the Seven Sages,
148c–d). 35 Ibid., 26.
36 Ibid., 40.

mêtis is

apatê *duplicity, deceit* [s.]

    simulation / dissimulation

        "the art of seeing without being seen"

    octopus

        takes the shape of the bodies to which it clings [t.]

        secretes cloud of ink

            to elude its enemies and to capture adversaries

        "These creatures so rich in **mêtis** can only be taken by their own traps: to catch them, fishermen throw them as bait a female of their own kind which they then grasp so tightly that nothing but death can make them let go."[32]

mêtis is

dokeuein *keen discernment, foresight*

    "Engaged in the world of becoming and confronted with situations which are ambiguous and unfamiliar and whose outcome always lies in the balance, wily intelligence is only able to maintain its hold over beings and things thanks to its ability to look beyond the immediate present and foresee a greater or lesser section of the future."[33]

mêtis is

kerdos *profit-gaining scheme*

    commercial

    mêtis architecture knows how to make a profit

mêtis is

kairos *opportune moment, bull's eye*

    the ability to seize an opportunity

mêtis is

haimulioi logoi *wily words*

    "Eumetis [daughter of a Greek philosopher], who knows how to resolve ambiguous words as well as twist them skilfully together is like Hephaestus and Hermes in that she possesses the double power of acting both as a bond and as a circle. Through her riddles she unfolds the endless cycle of her changing forms and with her subtle solutions she weaves around her questioners the same impassable circle that the hero who triumphs over the enigma binds about the elusive gods."[34]

Wily intelligence possesses the most prized cunning of all: the duplicity of the trap which always presents itself as what it is not and which conceals the true lethal nature beneath a reassuring exterior. [35]

It is this ability of the octopus and the **polutropos** one, the man of a thousand tricks, to assume every form without becoming imprisoned within any, that characterizes supple **mêtis** which appears to bow before circumstances only so that it can dominate them more surely. [36]

s.

t.

As the transforming form common to all architectural work, ***mêtis*** is not the invention of any period or the mark of any style. It is to be found with the architecture of the Aristotelian gaze in all the varieties of marriage. I end by tracing the particular coupling of Artemisia and Aristotle in two works of Scogin Elam and Bray: the Bridge at Concourse and the Clayton County Library. Each projects builds in its own way the "circular reciprocity between what is bound and what is binding."

37 *Architecture and Urbanism* 230 (November 1989): 85.

38 *Architectural Record* 176, no. 10 (September 1988): 115.

BRIDGE AT CONCOURSE

Proceeding genealogically from Artemisia via the Mausoleum and other tombs, we arrive at the Bridge at Concourse. The architects classify the Bridge as a folly, thus maintaining an opposition claimed by the client between desire and necessity and aligning the project with the marked/unmarked opposition in Classical typology between folly and architecture [u.]. In their project description they also acknowledge the inherited ambiguity of the folly—at once both a "house of pleasure" (like the Folies Bergères) and a monument of madness. They write:

> The bridge is an object in the landscape. It connects two points. It is about the desire to connect two points rather than the need to connect two points. It is a folly, an object of pleasure and enjoyment; an unreasonable combination of bridge parts, unnecessary and suggestive, demanding the attention of the crosser.[37]

The client, they further explain, asked for "a piece of jewelry" on the landscape, itself a man-made lagoon at the center of a super-corporate park.[38]

What the client desires, in other words, is a work in which the mechanisms of Artemisian **mêtis** serve to support Aristotelian hierarchy: necessity over desire, architecture over folly, clothing, over jewelry or its architectural counterpart, cladding over ornament or decoration. Scogin Elam and Bray might seem to have devoted themselves to satisfying their client's desire "uncritically"—that is, without discerning or promoting the discernment of that desire's necessity.

The Bridge is indeed a construction of **mêtis**. It thematizes **technê** *craft, skill* in a weaving of metalwork and carpentry and **apatê** *duplicity, deceit* in carpentry disguised as metalwork and cables and overscaled trusses without structural function, an apparent embodiment of unnecessary architectural desire. Especially when viewed from one of the surrounding high rises, it "shifts its shape" from bridge to dragonfly [v.].

With all these visual allurements, the Bridge functions, like the Classical folly of the British country estate, as an "eye-catcher"—commanding the gaze and answering it with a clear mark of place. As eye-catcher the folly confirms the ontological basis of Aristotelian knowledge: that something is there where you see it, replacing and placing everything

On the tradition of the architectural folly, see Anthony Vidler, "History of the Folly," in *Follies: Architecture for the Late-Twentieth-Century Landscape,* ed. B. J. Archer (New York: Rizzoli, 1983), 10-13. See also George Mott and Sally Aall, *Follies and Pleasure Pavillions: England, Ireland, Scotland, Wales* (New York: Abrams, 1989); Clay Lancaster, *Architectural Follies in America or Hammer, Saw, Tooth & Nail* (Rutland, Charles E. Tuttle, 1960); and Barbara Jones, *Follies and Grottoes* (London: Constable and Co., 1953).

v.   u.

else in its place. With its abundance of centering pieces and its symmetrical wings, this Bridge would seem to do nothing more than prove the unambiguous existence of a unique spatio-temporal centerpoint, and thereby the distinctions of aristocracy, be they social, architectural, cultural, or corporate.

In fulfilling the function of eye-catching folly, however (the function that would exclude necessity), and by the "Classic" gesture of *mêtis* (that is, imitating defeat), the Bridge reverses the subordination of folly to architecture. It works this reversal with an architectural joke and slip whose import, like that of many jokes and slips, may be unconscious. The Bridge does, as the architects say, "demand the attention of the crosser."

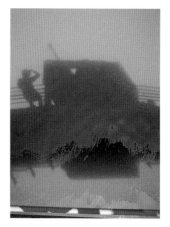

39 *Architecture and Urbanism* 230 (November 1989): 85.

40 Ibid.

So mount the Bridge and look again at that centerpoint. The boulder and vertical pole, precarious and extraneous, make the center a sign of irrationality, a focus of the folly as unanalyzed madness. First, as the architects themselves observe, the boulder "which should logically be a part of the abutments or the arch, presses downward at the midpoint, the point highest above the water."[39] In fact, it is attached to look as if it is rolling out from the Bridge and is about to fall off, taking the Bridge with it or letting the weight of the wings pull the structure down on the other side. The centerpoint turns into a "still unravaged bride" of collapse, a crazy bridge before which every crosser should hesitate.

Then, when you get to it, to quote the architects again, that "centerpoint displaces the person and causes movement along the short axis," that is, you are forced to "walk a perimeter around the

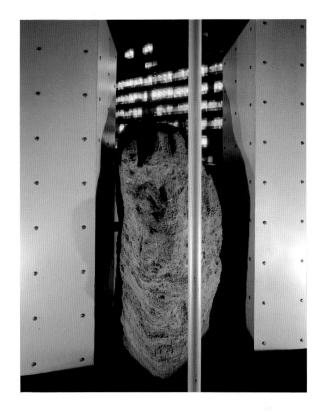

center."[40] The **mêtis** of the Bridge manifests itself as **haimulioi logoi** *wily words* that echo the name of the site, the "Perimeter Center" of Atlanta, and foster consideration of what the name might mean. The name "Perimeter Center" is a motivated accident, given before the Bridge was built and before the development of Concourse, but marking, as does the bridge [w.], the mobility, the subjectivity, the conjunction of centers—the **mêtis** of "center lines." In the context of the Bridge's reversability, the name also admits a check upon formal duplicity, since it itself is not reversable—"Center Perimeter" won't compute. The name of the site justifies the centering of perimeter but refuses the perimetering of the center.

Once you have made it across the Bridge, the tension of this material wordplay may elicit "attention" to the project's other "wily word." Why does the developer of a corporate park named "Concourse" *desire* a piece of jewelry in the form of a bridge? What **kerdos**, what profit is there for Concourse in connecting two points that do not have to be joined? The answer declares

The bridge is a conservative structure. Compare the title of the chief priest at Rome, the Pontifex (*bridge-maker*) Maximus. The Bridge conserves centers by troping perimeters. As a figure of **mêtis**, just by turning in one direction, it turns in the other.

w.

the necessity of desire. The Concourse requires the Bridge in order to be a "concourse"—a place that "flows together" with a point of perspective upon its buildings and man-made lake. The Concourse needs an eye-catcher in order to make it an eye-catcher.

Such is one of the meanings engendered by the choice of materials for the Bridge's wings. It could be claimed that the metal bars, both horizontal and vertical, lack the transparency and lightness necessary to embody the wings of a dragonfly folly. But when viewed in the light of the high rises opposite, the wings of the "jewel" reflect the strips of the "cladding." The relation of replacement between architecture and folly turns into reflection and refraction.

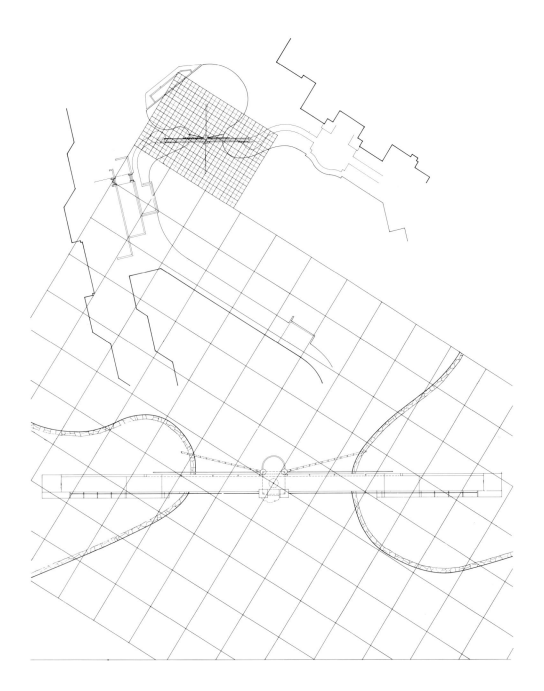

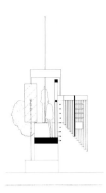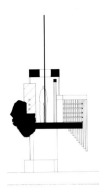

41 Heraclitus,
Fragment 93,
Die Fragmente der Vorsokratiker,
ed. Hermann Diels and Walther Kranz
(Berlin: Weidmann, 1951),
vol.1, p.172.

120

CLAYTON COUNTY LIBRARY

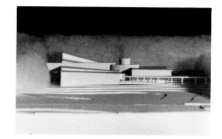

At the oracle of Apollo in Delphi, it is a female—the Pythia—who utters the words of the god in an oracle that, as Heraclitus says (Fragment 93),[41] neither *speaks* **legei** nor *conceals* **kruptei**, but **semainei** *speaks in signs*. And in Merrill Elam's description of Jonesboro, the site of the Library, during her 1989 lecture at SCI-Arc, I hear the signs of the Pythia. First:

> They have a peculiar way of seeing things in Jonesboro. If you live in Jonesboro and sit on your front porch, that's how you'll see your neighbor's house across the street because the railroad goes right through the middle of town—now that may have something to do with the kind of library they're willing to build in their communities.

What is this "way of seeing things?" What coupling of Aristotle and Artemisia engenders this "Jonesboro gaze?"[x.] When people look across the street, what do they see? Aristotle on the top and Artemisia on the bottom? Above, they see a triangular pedimental gable and pedimental window and door frames, a relic of the Classical desires of Southern gentry. Below, they see a bank covering the rest of the house. But no one in the house—on either side of the street—can be seen seeing. The viewers are covered, as they look at the face of middle-to-low-mimetic Classicism.

Listen again. After describing the town as the "mythical home of *Gone with the Wind*," Merrill says of Jonesboro: "on top of being Tara-ized, it's been commercialized"[y.] [z.]. "Tara-ized," in Merrill's lovely Southern accent, is almost indistinguishable from "terrorized." Merrill continues:

> You might also think that this was a strange place to have a fairly sophisticated client, but what happens in Jonesboro, Georgia is that it's the stopping place and the home town for lots of airline industry people, and the Chairman of the Board of Trustees; here was an ex-pilot and he had almost died at one point in his career in a crash—so risk-taking for him was on an entirely different level than it might be for some other clients that we've all worked with.

What does this "Jonesboro gaze"—this Tara-izing—what does being a death-defying pilot have to do with the library that Scogin Elam and Bray have built? To decipher this riddle, look at the coupling of Artemisia and Aristotle in the building itself.

This library may be one of the "foxiest" and "frog-fishiest" architectures ever built. The skin is

x.

y. z.

utterly **pantoie** *multiple* and **poikile** *variegated*. It is a tricky **mechanê** *artifice* of metalwork, an **apatê** simulating and dissimulating low-mimetic material and high-mimetic art. It is corrugated metal treated with exacting **technê** *craft*. It is the cover of a library box executed in grand, pointillistic sweeps. With **dokeuein** *keen critical discernment* of its social **kairos** *opportunity*, it speaks the **hiamulioi logoi** *wily words* of black and white integration. This is the "new South"—the "air-conditioned South"—where lynchings and long, hot summers are things of the past. This "small town" is part of the "global village." Men here fly all over the country, no longer fixed to the tensions of the soil.

In accord with this context, as Artemisia dressed her troops in the costumes of their enemies so they would admit them into their city, so the Library sheds all trace of the uncritical Classicism that covers so many public libraries in favor of a nonthreatening literacy, nonchalance, and architectural fantasy. A parodic propylon supports an overscaled sign that doesn't seem to know—or better, doesn't seem to care—about the difference between "capitals" and lower-case letters. In carefree release from rectilinear containment and inanimation, the building breathes in and

42 *Progressive Architecture*
(November 1988),
82.

raises its roof, like wings captured in stop-action photography. In elevation, especially at night, they are transparent, like insect's wings, a ***mêtis*** that turns the dappled skin of the building into a trope of the body of a dragonfly, like those you can see in the woods beside it. "Real architecture" here becomes stylish, ingratiating, techno- and zoomorphic folly. It won't be a "drag" to read in here. Imitating the defeat of high-cultural control, the Clayton County Library puts on the face of a hip "K-Mart for Information."[42] The "captured insect" lures its prey inside. This library is a master, or should we say mistress, of low-cost, high-volume ***kerdos*** *profit*.

Once inside, the Library retains its patrons with a series of "metistic" amenities constructed at the apparent cost of purity of plan. Risking the loss of Classical control, the ambiguous cruciform/H-form plan includes underscaled protrusions—little warts, if the plan were a body. These awkward adjacencies combine with the asymmetrical flanks and the uncertainty of axial hierarchy to create the ruse of aesthetic accident. The plan seems ready to sacrifice Aristotelian values in service of an Artemisian success, satisfying the desires of adults, with cozy, train-compartment reading carrels (signaled with inverted wishbone ducting subliminally recalling the triangular gable of the Jonesboro gaze), of children, with a little story-telling amphitheater all their own, and of staff members, with triangular offices looking out into the woods. The plan provides pleasurable, private space, where it is possible to gaze Jonesboro-style with the sense of enclosure, of not being seen. The plan seems willing to deny itself composite elegance and Classical integration in order to create inviting, partial enclaves—spaces that "work well as parts" but detract from the "working" of the scheme as a whole.

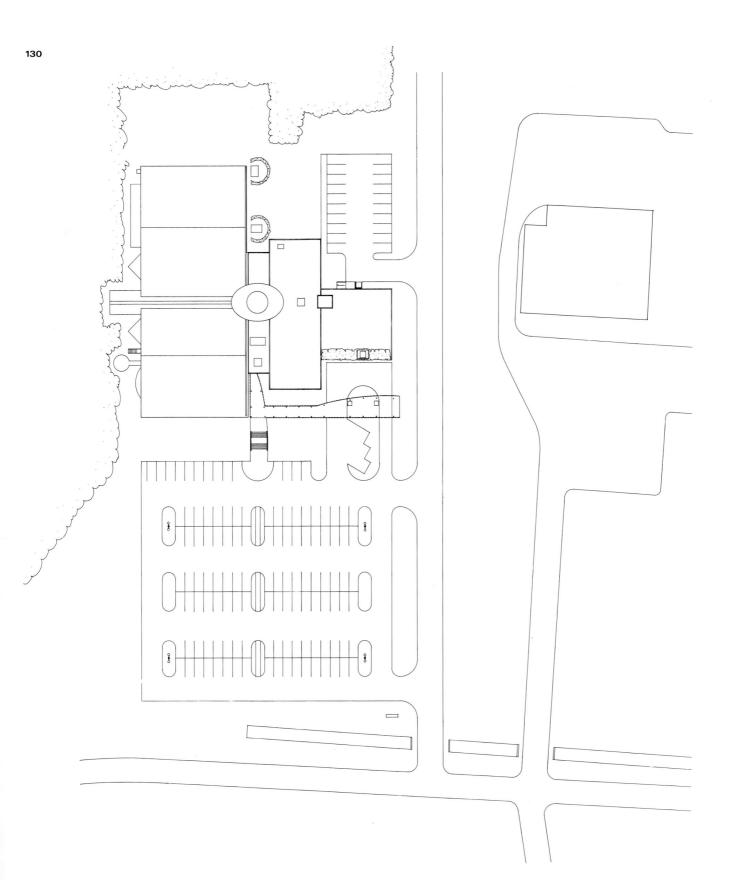

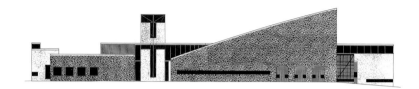

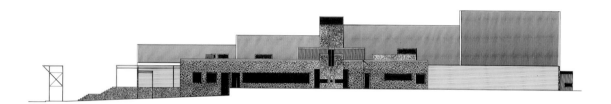

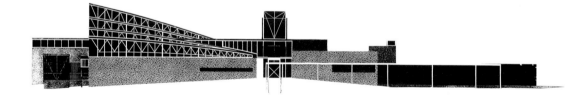

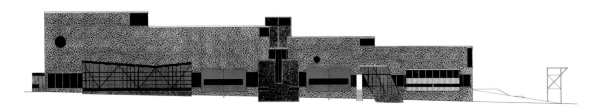

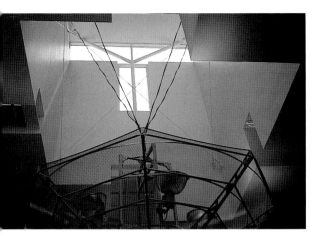

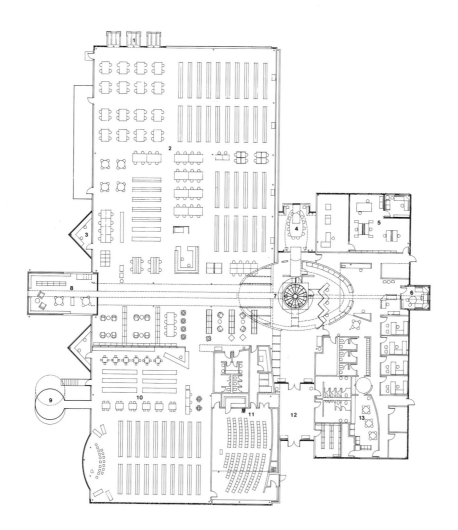

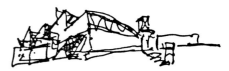

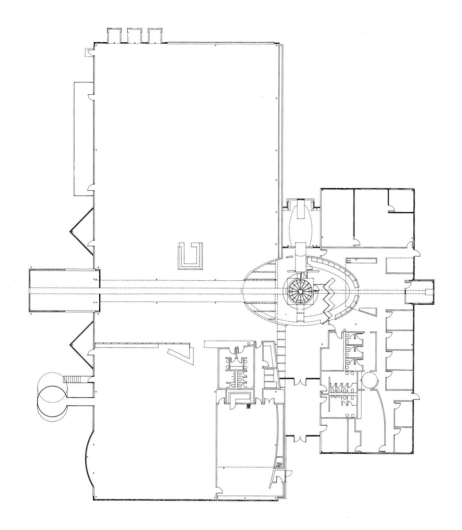

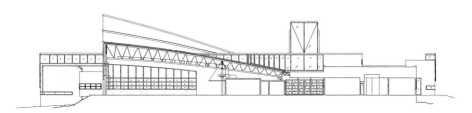

Such a critical assessment of the Jonesboro gaze, its Tara-ization, and the lack of "fear of flying" here is not wrong but is rather itself only partial. It underestimates the "working" of the couple, Artemisia and Aristotle, in this building, and the "circular reciprocity between what is bound and what is binding." As the fox-fish turns its body inside out, so that the interior becomes exterior and the hook falls out, as the fishing frog dangles its linelike tongue as bait, so the plan of the Clayton County Library turns into a structure of Classical surveillance and social control. The folly of the captured insect turns inside out to expose a web in which "metistic" lures position the subject for architecture's inherited role as builder of political philosophy.

Far from mitigating the working of Classical order, the Library's foxy attractions draw people to places where they feel private—feel they are not seen seeing—but in fact can be surveyed by all who travel along the building's lateral axis. This relation between vision and knowledge is symbolized by the dominant *architectural* gesture of extending the sight line through a porthole from the Director's office along the whole length of this axis—itself accentuated with a fishing line of white neon, turned into an inverted aisle of light by elongated soffits and clerestory windows, and sublimated at the central dome and endpoints into cruciform "light monitors"—to the Genealogy room at the other end. There so fervently does the Library inculcate the principle of knowledge as visual that the books float above the floor-level light of the mind.

The Library circulates its knowledge at the intersection of its axes where visibility is most complete. Despite its deployment under an ellipse (the figure composed of two circles whose centerlines never meet), this Circulation desk remains monocular, commanding the middle, a "golden mean" crowned with light.

In its most panoptic vision, the Jonesboro gaze discerns a region where the Artemisian troping of racial, sexual, and social hierarchy, where the folly defusing the passion and violence anticipated by us who look in from outside, and where the architectural **mêtis** that shapes the political agenda and the artifices of corporate grandeur in the new South is itself encircled by the Aristotelian eye [Ω.].

VIDLER *Merrill, for years I have been a very, very respectful and close reader of feminist criticism. But I have always been admonished by Linda Nochlin, who is an art historian, that feminist criticism ought not to be just one other instrument that you would add to the hegemonic criticism. This is really the first time that looking at a body of work has forced me to try to reconstruct a complex idea like ornament through the lens of feminism, and I suspect it has to do with something in the work that I am noticing.*

ELAM *I was hoping you wouldn't ask that. Actually, even the term feminist criticism is . . .*

VIDLER *I know, it's difficult.*

ELAM *Yeah, because I am not a scholar. I don't understand that whole package of information. I think it is not a conscious thing. I'm sure from now on you'll ask that question more often, and I won't be able to use this answer again. But I would like to say something else about criticism in general and this forum today. My thought is for this community. If we are a community of practitioners and scholars who can come together in a kind of critical dialogue, we'll go away a much stronger community because there is that sort of critical dialogue that will allow us to back away from our work and get reinvolved in the work in a different way. I was terrorized by Alan's use of the word "style." So we're going to think about that, I can assure you. On the other hand, Ann's reading of the architecture was a revelation for me.*

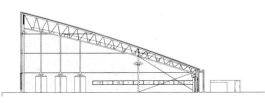

WQXI RADIO

142

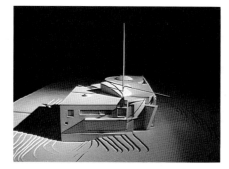

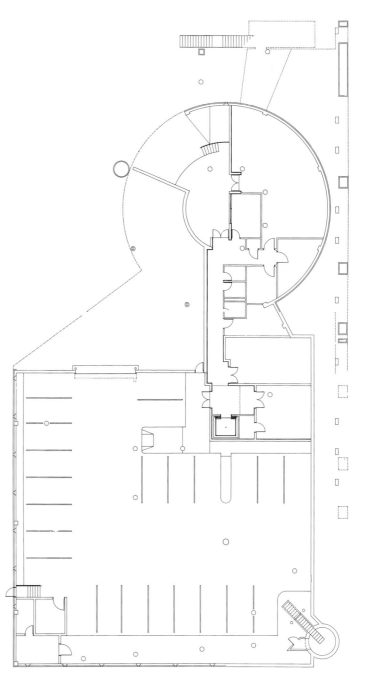

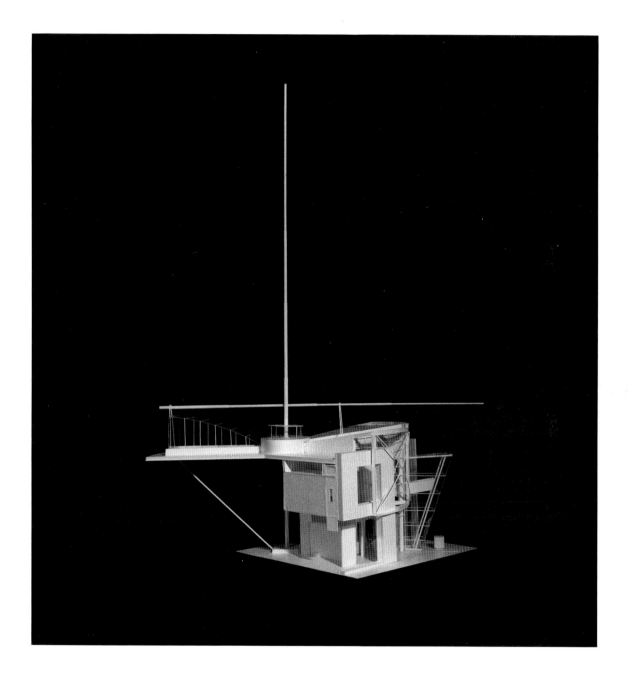

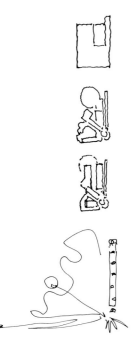

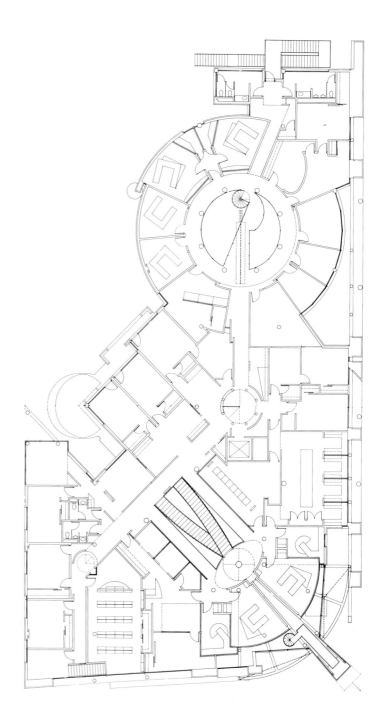

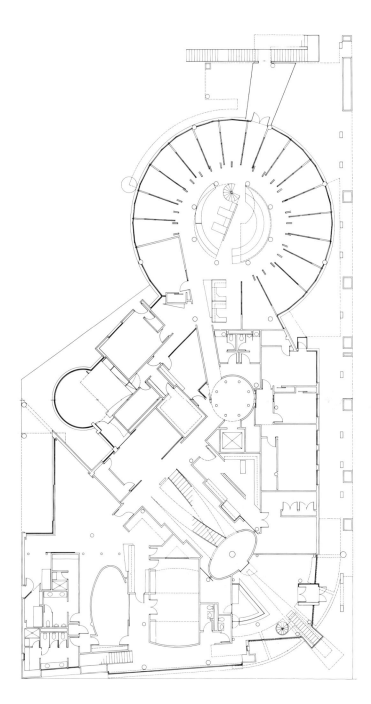

Dressing Down: Monuments and Material Cladding

Anthony Vidler

In the last twenty years the criticism of the worst results of a modernism dedicated to technological and capital development, like that of the Modern Movement in the twenties and thirties, has been divided politically and formally. The tempered modification of the modern, recognizing the disastrous effects of urban renewal—the "Athens Charter" effect—has sustained a neorationalist, typological, and critically protechnological position against a neotraditionalism that at its most radical has advocated a return to medieval and antique methods of construction. At its worst, this debate over the form and method of constructing urbanity has degenerated into stylistic battles reminiscent of the nineteenth century—the techno-topians versus the neoclassicists. Each position has sought authority in history, whether that of the early twentieth century or earlier; each has elaborated the political and cultural implications of its spatial and ornamental credo.

From the standpoint of the late twentieth century such debates might be construed as mere extensions of the long tradition of "theoretical practice," forged with the instruments of representation and technique invented by the Renaissance and renewed with modern vigor as tools of Enlightenment and historicist progress. From the late eighteenth century on the debates for and against the city (whether conducted by means of utopian propositions or reformist solutions) have formed a litany of project and counter-project, only broken by the efforts of revolutionaries and avant-gardes to force an absolute rupture with the past at all costs. In this frame of reference, late-twentieth-century disputes over the nature of ornament, the formal vocabulary of architecture, appropriate technological responses, or the politics of style might seem historically insignificant or at least artificial. With historical distance even the now discredited utopianism of the early avant-gardes seems more "authentic" than its replication by contempory architects.

A culturally responsive criticism, however, is bound to respond to difference as well as to similarity; the repetition of history is never as simple as surface appearances indicate. Accordingly, as a critical historian I am drawn to identify not only the obvious burdens of influence, traditional or avant-garde, in contemporary work but also the precise and specific differences—of contexts and objects—that mark the present from its apparent roots.

The work of Scogin Elam and Bray affords an especially rewarding subject in this regard. Their wide-ranging knowledge of modernist precedent, consciously posed against revivalist postmodernism, serves as a statement of the continuing verities of the modern; it nevertheless, in context and subject matter, programs and their formal resolutions, stands equally for difference and contemporaneity. Thus, as the architects themselves point out in the context of the Clayton County Headquarters Library, their architecture is as much a response to the "folksy" hand-painted strip and a conception of "library" as "filling station for information" as it is a more general commentary on the nature of modernist architecture. This dual concern is also apparent in two buildings that are

1 Sigfried Giedion,
"The Need for a New
Monumentality,"
Harvard Architecture Review 4
(Spring 1984):
53–54.

2 José Luis Sert, Fernand Léger,
and Sigfried Giedion,
"Nine Points on Monumentality,"
Harvard Architecture Review 4
(Spring 1984):
63.

less charged with cultural connotations: the Buckhead Library—situated in a refurbished, affluent section of Atlanta—and the High Museum at Georgia Pacific—sequestered in the base of a corporate office tower downtown. Each of these buildings is both tied into and distinct from its context, and each is responsively attentive to the contemporary vocabulary of modernist style.

Following the lead of these filiations and differences, I would like to concentrate for a moment on one particular aspect of this double focus of criticism, modernist and contextual: the intriguing relationship between *monumentality* and *ornament*. Both have had a difficult intellectual history in modernist theory: the general attack of the avant-gardes was against monumentality (at least of the nineteenth-century, Beaux-Arts kind), and more often than not it was also against ornament. If a "new monumentality" was theorized as, for example, by Sigfried Giedion, it was based on the morality of functional presence—the building standing for what it housed without added rhetoric —and if ornament was envisaged as anything other than crime, it was to be derived from the technological determinants of construction or formal abstraction [a.].

The question of ornament appears especially problematic today, when traditionalist postmodernism, dedicated to the restoration of humanist architectural details, is being countered by what seems to be an equally nostalgic revival of modernism's own motifs. The paradox is clear: modernism, in stylistic terms, signaled "no ornament," yet the "signs" or motifs of modernism now being displayed have apparently reached the very point of becoming no more than ornament. The condition is the same whether we speak of the "constructivist" references of Tschumi, the "neo-fifties" quotes of Koolhaas, or the apparently more complicated "deconstructions" of Coop Himmelblau, Daniel Libeskind, and Peter Eisenman. Indeed, the very notion of ornament is, in many contemporary projects, thrown into doubt, as the traditional distinction between that which is essential and that which is auxiliary (a distinction that was a necessary condition of "postmodern" irony) is blurred or discarded altogether.

As "auxiliary light and complement to beauty," in Alberti's terms, ornament presupposes the existence of an original and originating body: hence the organic analogies of classicism and the sartorial analogies of eclecticism and modernism. Without such bodies, whether symbolic or

All of us are perfectly aware of the fact that monumentality is a dangerous affair in a time when most of the people do not even grasp the elementary requirements for a functional building. . . . This is the period of psuedo-monumentality. The greater part of the nineteenth century belongs to it. The models of the past were not imbued, as in the Renaissance, with a strong artistic vision leading to new results. There was a helpless undirected and, at the same time routine use of shapes from bygone periods. They were used indiscriminately everywhere, for any kind of building. Because they had lost their inner significance, they had become devaluated, mere clichés without emotional justification. . . . Architects found traces of the undisguised expression of their period far removed from monumental edifices. They found them in the market halls, in factories, in the bold vaulting problems of the great exhibition buildings, or in the only real monument of this period, the Eiffel Tower (1889). There was no denying that they lacked the splendor of buildings of bygone periods, which had been nourished by handicraft and a long tradition. They were naked and rough, but they were true. Nothing else could have served as the point of departure for a language of our own.[1]

Modern materials and new techniques are at hand: light metal structures; curved, laminated wooden arches; panels of different textures, colors, and sizes; light elements like ceilings which can be suspended from big trusses covering practically unlimited spans. . . . Mobile elements can constantly vary the aspect of the buildings. These mobile elements, changing positions and casting different shadows when acted upon by wind or machinery, can be the source of new architectural effects.[2]

a.

3 Gianni Vattimo,
The End of Modernity
(Baltimore: Johns Hopkins
University Press, 1988),
87.

4 Vattimo,
The End of Modernity,
87–88.

148

structural, the condition for ornament seems absent. Thus where, for example, a facade by Michael Graves, Charles Moore, or Robert Venturi goes to great lengths to distinguish between ornament and what is being ornamented, the facadeless grids and colliding forms of the deconstructivists seem at once to discard all ornament and to become entirely ornamental.

Here the traditional identification of ornament with its proximity to the architectural "body" breaks down before the apparent paradox of a building comprised of "total ornament"—which immediately poses the question: "Ornament to what?" That is, with respect to what entity larger than architecture itself is architecture ornamental? A comparison between the evidently decorative role of materials in the Buckhead Library and the equally evident rejection of all materiality in the recently completed Wexner Center for the Visual Arts at Ohio State University, by Eisenman and Trott, illustrates the difference nicely. At the Buckhead Library surfaces are carefully articulated in pattern, color, and texture to reveal the deliberate "difference" between surface and structure; at the Wexner Center, by contrast, the obviously ornamental grid that fills the passage between the Center and the adjoining building and the equally "ornamental" grids that pattern the floors and walls of the Center proper are deliberately confused in their roles. Ostensibly ornamental, these constructed and inlaid grids are, in fact, simply extensions and manifestations of grids that compose the whole building, itself formed out of collisions among at least three grids of different scales, themselves derived from virtual and real grids that map the context. In this situation, if we draw the conventional distinction between ornament and nonornament, we may on the one hand conclude that Scogin Elam and Bray are simply exacerbating a traditional split, making a virtue out of necessity, so to speak, in ways forged by Venturi and Scott Brown among others; on the other hand, we may interpret the Wexner Center and other similar buildings in terms of a triumphant and totalizing ornamentalism.

If, however, we turn to the Italian philosopher Gianni Vattimo's reading of the late Heidegger, we are drawn to conclude that both Scogin Elam and Bray and Eisenman may be, consciously or unconsciously, trapped in what he calls a "post-historical" condition of "weak monumentality," producing an essentially ornamental art that holds a "background" position as an assertion of the marginal become central. Against the strong metaphysical, monumental tradition of the Hegelian utopia, such monuments, in Vattimo's terms, provide "a backdrop to which no attention is paid, and . . . a surplus which has no possible legitimation in an authentic foundation."[3] For Vattimo, "What is lost in the foundation and ungrounding which is ornament, is the heuristic and critical function of the distinction between decoration as surplus and what is 'proper' to the thing and to the work,"[4] that is, the distinction between essence and auxiliary. This loss, or "exhaustion" is, in Vattimo's conclusion, acknowledged in the monument become ornament, invaded by the very

BUCKHEAD LIBRARY

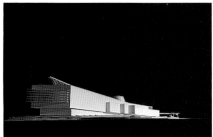

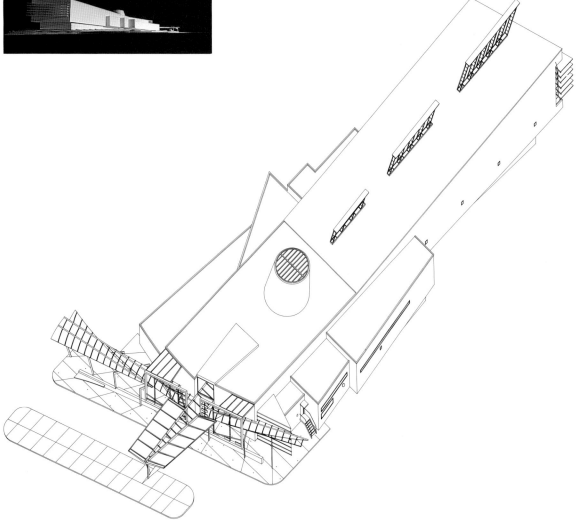

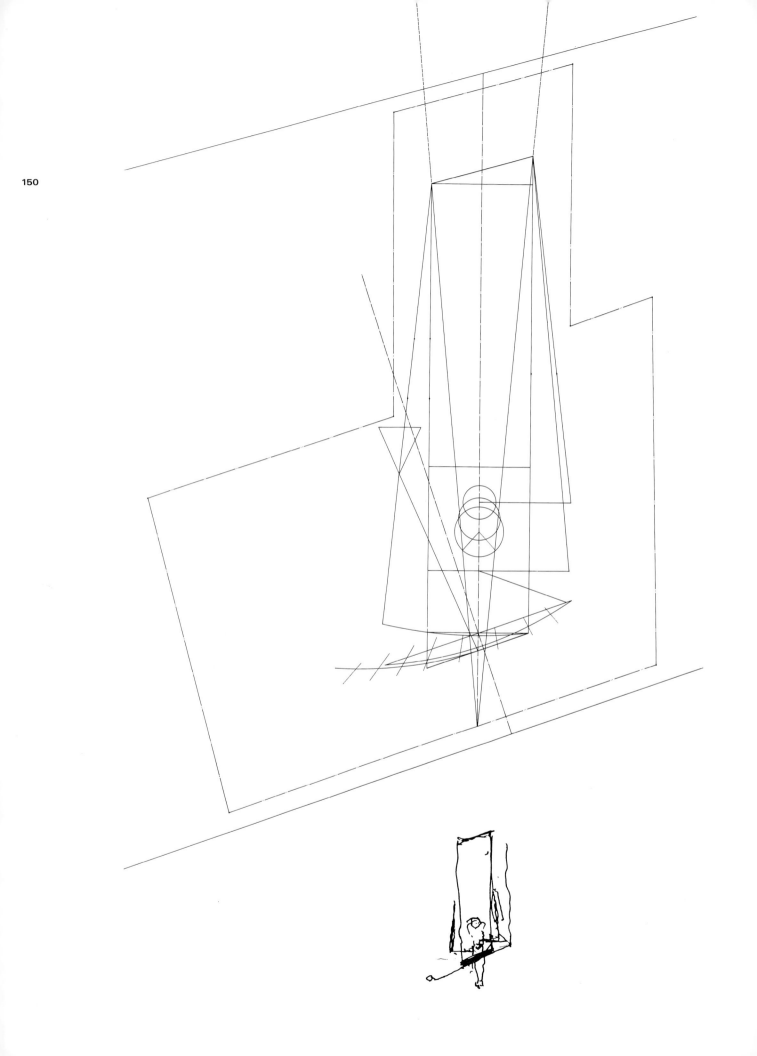

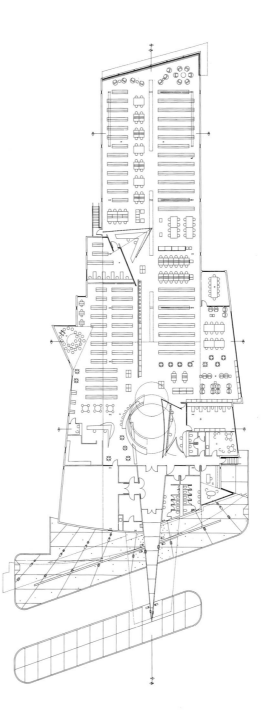

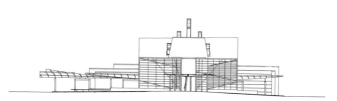

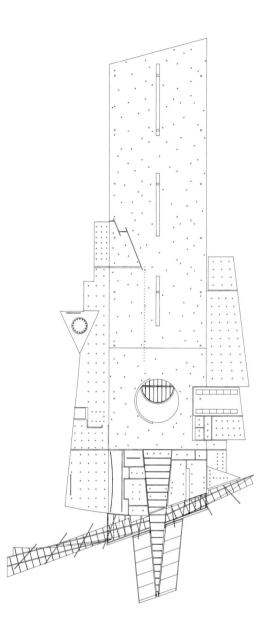

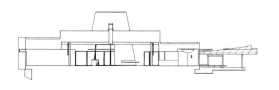

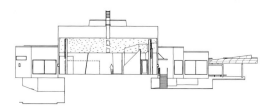

5 Georg W.F. Hegel,
Aesthetics. Lectures on Fine Art,
trans. T. M. Knox, (Oxford:
Oxford University Press, 1975),
vol. 1, p. 423.

6 John Whiteman,
"On Hegel's Definition of Architecture,"
Assemblage 2 (February 1987):
10, 13.

surplus that was, originally, its reason for being.

Yet however tempting this notion of the monument as "residue" of memory, as already ruined trace, as "pure" decoration might be, we should perhaps stop at the easy equivalence posed by "counter-monuments," whether of the type of the Buckhead Library or of the Wexner Center, and the philosophy of a Heidegger recuperated for post-history and counter-nostalgia. Rather, the evident monumentality and presence of such buildings—a presence to which works as diverse as Libeskind's Berlin Wall project, Coop Himmelblau's rooftop schemes in Vienna, and Venturi and Scott Brown's recent buildings on the campus of Princeton University, also aspire—clearly indicates a *desire* for the essential that far surpasses any ironic backgrounding or fatigued playing. In all of the so-called "deconstructive" or "postmodern" projects, indeed, hovers the trace not of an exhausted memory but of an active and dialectical opposition that tends not so much to a weakened monumentality as to a new kind of monumentality.

The theoretical conditions for interpreting such "totalizations" of ornament can be constructed more out of the fault lines of post-Hegelian attempts to *recuperate* monumentality than of "post-historical" philosophies of loss or failure. In this sense, we can begin to articulate the conditions for a monumental ornament that has no need of the original monument, an ornament, in other words, that takes its definition from what it implies rather than from that to which it is added. Hegel, in his paradoxical formulation of the dilemma of architecture, already points to this condition. In his discussion of the disappearance of the symbolic form of art, to which, as we know, architecture fundamentally belongs, Hegel speaks of the moment when the symbol, dedicated to the perfect unity of inner meaning and external shape, is undermined by the classical will to use and dominate according to a strict separation of means and ends. His example is that of didactic poetry, where the content is entirely developed in its "prosaic" form to the extent that any artistic shape imposed on this form is external and ornamental. "What has become prosaic in itself," he concludes, "is not to be reshaped poetically; it can only be dressed up; just as horticulture, for example, is for the most part just an external arrangement of a site already given by nature and not in itself beautiful, or as architecture by ornament and external decoration makes pleasant the utility of premises devoted to prosaic circumstances and affairs."[5] In these terms, Hegel maintains, didactic poetry and, by direct implication, architecture, "cannot be numbered amongst the proper forms of art." We are presented, then, with an art—architecture—the first of all the arts, symbolic in its essence, that *essentially* cannot remain symbolic, that must become prosaic and therefore entirely ornamental. Or, in reverse, we are presented with a notion of ornament that, once distinguished *as* ornament, separately from the essential symbol, undermines the symbolic equation of form and content, fatally marking architecture for an unhappy death long before all of the other arts [b.].

For Hegel, architecture, far from being timid about its symbolic power (a characteristic of the thought of our time), is so powerful that it is likely to become "over-real." . . . Hegel's analysis of architecture suggests that we must tackle what appears to us as architecture's "original sin"—that it is most powerful when it concerns itself with "mere appearance" and, in doing so, becomes inescapably rhetorical. We have been scared away from the real power of architecture, its symbolic power. [6]

b.

7 Gottfried Semper,
"Development of Architectural Style,"
trans. J. W. Root, *The Inland Architect
and News Record* 14, no. 7
(December 1889):
77.

8 Gottfried Semper,
"Style in the Technical and Techtonic Arts
or Practical Aesthetics," *The Four
Elements of Architecture and Other Writings,*
trans. Harry Mallgrave and Wolfgang Herrmann
(Cambridge: Cambridge University Press, 1989),
254.

Perhaps in the light of such a fatality we can read the post-Hegelian attempts to reconstitute the nature of ornament as an organic extension of bodily display, as so many theoretical expressions of a need to reconstitute monumentality, but now *as* dress. With no pretense to the symbolic, a monument can take on the role of the sign, always assuming that the true nature of this sign—its arbitrariness—can be distinguished at first glance. Ornament thus becomes a proper subject for enquiry on its own terms and is seen, anthropologically and sociologically, as a direct outgrowth of the same instincts for tatooing, ritual dressing, and the wearing of jewelry that constitute society itself. In these terms ornament can even be construed as the very foundation of architectural style.

Gottfried Semper's construction of an architecture that owes its origin to the adornment of the body seems in retrospect a means of recuperating architecture once more, this time not as symbol but as ornament—"adornment is the first important step toward art: in adornment and its laws is contained the complex codex of formal esthetics." For Semper all of architecture's decorative elements—those that accentuate the relations of the parts of the structure, those that designate distinctions among the parts, those that point to the purpose of the building and, finally, those that relate the work to the universe as a whole—originate in the adornment of the body and its extensions in the industry of the family. Adornment is what distinguishes the human species from all animals, it was what marked the striving for individuality: "By adorning anything, be it alive or inanimate, I bestow upon it the right of individual life. By making it the center of relations that pertain to it alone, I elevate it to the rank of a person."[7] Hence the principle of "dressing," or *Bekleidung*, which Semper identifies *first* in architecture, then as a distinguishing mark for the body:

> The art of dressing the body's nakedness (if we do not count the ornamental painting of one's own skin) is probably a later invention than the use of coverings for encampments and spatial enclosures. There are tribes whose savagery appears to be the most primitive, who do not know clothing, yet to whom the use of skins and even a more or less developed industry of spinning, plaiting, and weaving for the furnishing and security of their encampments is not unknown.[8]

9 Semper,
"Development of an Architectural Style,"
252.

Ornament, from a mere auxiliary, emerges as *the* foundation of architecture, and dressing and incrustation become the means by which structure and the division of space are represented, linguistically and socially, as monumental form:

> This tradition of incrustation, in fact, applies to the totality of Hellenic art and prevails, above all, as the true essence of architecture. It limits itself in no way simply to a type of tendentious decorative adornment of surfaces with sculpture and painting, but essentially conditions the *art-form in general; in Greek architecture, both the art-form and decoration are so intimately bound together by this influence of the principle of surface dressing that an isolated look at either is impossible.*[9]

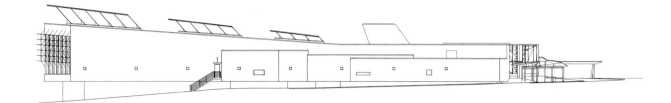

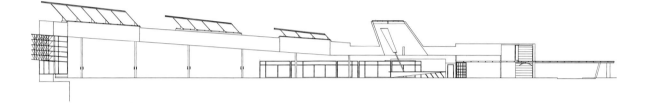

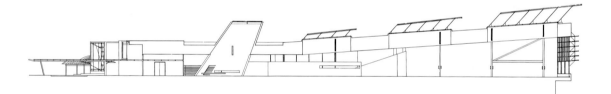

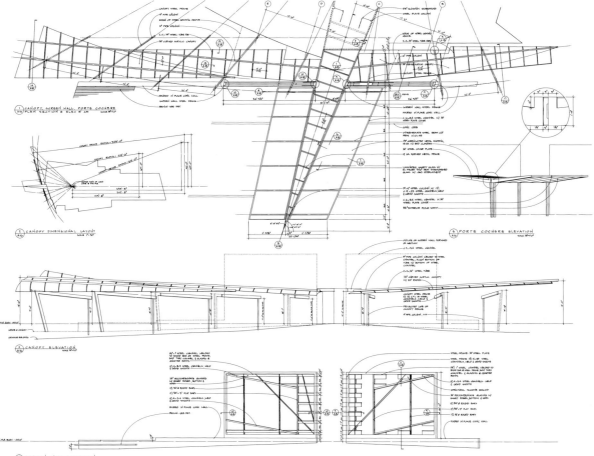

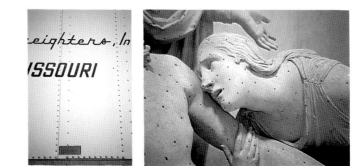

10 Adolf Loos,
    "Potemkin City," *Spoken into the Void:
    Collected Essays 1897–1900*,
    trans. Jane O. Newman and John H. Smith
    (Cambridge: MIT Press, 1982), 95–96.
    [First published in *Ver Sacrum* (July 1898).]

In this way, Semper counters the Hegelian "loss" of symbolic form by asserting the very primacy of dressing, for Hegel the symptom of division and decline.

In this light Adolf Loos's apparent "refusal" of ornament may be seen as the ethical corollorary of Semper's materialist justification. The force of what Loos calls the "principle of cladding" is directed against the "Potemkin City" of "canvas and pasteboard" with its historicist facades "nailed on" to structures whose real and truly modern identity is thereby hidden. Loos decries this city of frock coats and fur collars concealing social equals, a bourgeois city pretending to be a city of aristocrats.[10] Against this Loos called for an "authentic style" that proudly displays the "modernity" of techniques and life in the

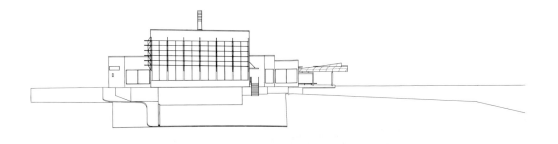

11 Adolf Loos,
"The Principle of Cladding,"
Spoken into the Void, 66–69.
[First published in the *Neue Freie Presse*, September 4, 1898.]

12 Adolf Loos,
"Ladies' Fashion,"
Spoken into the Void,
102.

late nineteenth century by openly revealing the distinction between structure and hung enclosure, by using materials that reveal their nature and a strict separation between "the material clad" and "cladding."[11]

Loos's sartorial ethics, summarized in the formula "ornament is something that must be overcome,"[12] do not by any means imply the total eradication of ornament but rather the eradication of ornament of another time, place, and role; the destruction of survivals, primitive and otherwise; the breaking down of prejudices in the same way, for example, that "the twentieth century woman cyclist" might "wear pants and clothing that leaves her feet free."

Modern architecture is thereby to be "dressed down" for action, and ornament becomes folded into the structure of the object. Identifying the tattoo as degenerate and criminal and concentrating his attack on dress, Loos shifts the argument from Semper's "tailorization" to modernist Taylorization. It was no accident that the 1908 essay "Ornament and Crime" appeared in its French translation in the same number of *L'Esprit Nouveau* as Le Corbusier's *éloge* to the Maisons Voisin, to the factory sheds and to *"la rhythmique"* of the new dance. It thus poses the question in precisely those Taylorist terms that Le Corbusier was advancing.

Loos's strident polemic has been usually summarized in terms of Freudian theories of primitivism and eroticism, with special focus on his sexual and anthropological arguments for the "degeneracy" of ornament. But when we read it in the light of theories of the division of labor and industrial efficiency, Loos's prose takes on a slightly different cast. His refusal of ornament seems not only to be based on quasi-Darwinian or Spencerian theories of racial progress or Freudian constructions of erotic desire but also and even primarily on a utilitarian argument: "The evolution of culture," he claims, "is synonymous with the removal of

13 Adolf Loos,
"Ornament and Crime" [1908]
in Ulrich Conrads, ed., *Programs
and Manifestoes on 20th-Century
Architecture*, trans. Michael Bullock
(Cambridge: MIT Press, 1975), 20.

14 Loos,
"Ornament and Crime,"
21.

15 Ibid.,
22.

16 Otto Wagner,
Modern Architecture,
trans. Harry Mallgrave.
(Santa Monica: The Getty Center, 1988),
60.

164

ornament from utilitarian objects."[13] Here the evolutionary historicism of the late nineteenth century is allied to an economics of production:

> The enormous damage and devastation caused in aesthetic development by the revival of ornament would be easily made light of, for no one, not even the power of the state, can halt mankind's evolution. . . . But it is a crime against the national economy that it should result in a waste of human labor, money and material. Time cannot make do this damage.[14]

"Ornament," he concludes, "inflicts serious injury on people's health, on the national budget and hence on cultural evolution: ornament is wasted labor power and hence wasted health."[15]

Thus fashion, which impels continuous changes of ornamental style, supports a consumption economy based on waste and obsolescence, leading to what Loos describes as "a premature devaluation of the labour product." In this cycle of production and consumption both the worker's time and the material employed are "capital goods that are wasted." Loos sounds almost Taylorist as he analyzes the benefits to worker and society of repudiating "ornament on things that have evolved away from the need to be ornamented." The wasted labor and ruined material saved by the suppression of ornament may be, so to speak, reinvested in both the worker and society. The worker, working a shorter time, nevertheless produces a more culturally durable, nonconsumable product. More durable, thus more valuable to society, this product may then be more expensive to buy. This will then lead to a higher reward for the worker who works for a shorter time *not* producing ornament and thence takes home a higher reward. Such a position might seem to anticipate both the notion of material as its own ornament (the Buckhead Library) and the idea of built structure as a total ornament in itself (the Wexner Center).

These principles of modern architecture themselves reflect the outline of modernity sketched by Loos's older contemporary Otto Wagner in his *Modern Architecture* of 1895, with its dramatic appeal "that the basis of today's predominant views on architecture must be shifted, we must become fully aware that the sole departure point for our artistic work can only be modern life."[16] Architecture might then throw off the clothes of the past, revealing the technical and social conditions of the present. Henceforth "nudity" would remain one of the leitmotivs of modernism, sometimes allying itself to a revival of that heroic neo-Hellenistic nudity celebrated by classicists from Winckelmann on, sometimes implying the total expression of psychological states in form.

In this regard it is interesting to remember that Georg Simmel, in his own treatment of adornment and ornament, places it in the realm of social distinguishing marks, seeing it as partaking of the same order of distinction, of drawing attention, as the secret. Adornment, "although apparently the sociological counter-pole of secrecy," has an analogous structure: even as it forms part of

[17] Georg Simmel, *The Sociology of Georg Simmel*, trans., ed., and introd. Kurt H. Wolff (New York: The Free Press, 1950), 344. [Originally published as "Exkurs über den Schmuck," *Soziologie, Untersuchungen über die Formen der Vergesellschaftung* (Leipzig, 1908).]

[18] Siegfried Kracauer, "The Mass Ornament," trans. and introd. Karsten Witte, *New German Critique* 5 (Spring 1985), 67–76.

[19] Simmel, *Sociology of George Simmel*, 340.

[20] Siegfried Kracauer, "Girls and Crisis," *Frankfurter Zeitung*, May 26, 1931. [Quoted in Karsten Witte, "Introduction to Siegfried Kracauer's 'The Mass Ornament,'" *New German Critique* 2 (1975): 63–64.]

[21] Georg Simmel, *The Philosophy of Money*, ed. David Frisby, trans. Tom Bottomore and David Frisby (Routledge: New York, 1990), 256.

the social structure of secrecy to engender envy and attention, so "it is the nature of adornment to lead the eyes of others upon the adorned." Such distinction would be entirely out of place in a Taylorist world without wasted time or ornament: "This environment looks with much less attention at the unadorned individual, and passes by without including him."[17] The secret, the adorned, the masked would, in any case, disrupt the total subordination of production and consumption to the managerial economies of time and space [c.].

On one level, of course, this restriction of ornament in building simply shifts the ornamental imperative onto society itself, creating the conditions for the production of what Simmel's student Siegfried Kracauer was to characterize as the "mass ornament," watchword of the *neue Sacklichkeit*, the new objectivity of architects from Hannes Meyer to Mies van der Rohe. Writing in 1927, Kracauer argues that the increasing lack of ornament in architecture is more and more compensated for by a new phenomenon—the ornament of the masses themselves, as exhibited in stadia and street. Thus the masses appear, with their regularity and pattern of bodies, *as* ornament: "The decisive agent of ornament is the mass"[18] [d.].

On another level, however, as Simmel himself intimates, ornament in architecture is simply displaced to a third and even more triumphant moment. As Simmel remarks:

> Everything that "adorns" man can be ordered along a scale in terms of its closeness to the physical body. The "closest" adornment is typical of nature peoples: tattooing. The opposite extreme is represented by metal and stone adornments, which are entirely individual and can be put on by everybody. Between these two stands dress, which is not so inexchangeable and personal as tattooing, but neither so un-individual and separable as jewelry, *whose very elegance lies in its impersonality.*[19]

In one sense the development of post-Hegelian architectural theory paralleled this movement: from the monument as binding meaning and form in the symbol, a monument that stood for the analogous human body, to the monument as distinguishing between essence and appearance through the clear play of the sign and standing for the "dressed" body, the possibility was open for the monument (as opposed to the unadorned structure of the prosaic mass-building) to be freed from any but representational use and thus to be seen as total ornament. If Loos restricts "Architecture" to the tomb and the monument, it is to return architecture, so to speak, to the "symbolic" realm, but now in the form of the completely superfluous, the triumphant mask.

As Simmel intimates, ornament is, as the mainspring of social distinction, that distinguishing mark that binds individuality to possession:

> As adornment usually is an object of considerable value, it is a synthesis of the individual's having and being; it

When they formed an undulating snake, they radiantly illustrated the virtues of the conveyor belt; when they tapped their feet in fast tempo, it sounded like *business, business*; when they kicked their legs high with mathematical precision they joyously affirmed the progress of rationalization; and when they kept repeating the same movements without ever interrupting their routine, one envisaged an uninterrupted chain of motor cars gliding from the factories into the world, and believed that the blessing of prosperity had no end. [20]

According to Simmel, the citizen forms a defensive *"blasé* attitude" due to the daily confrontation with repetition, similarity, and regularity. "The *blasé* person—although the concept of such a person is rarely fully realized—has completely lost the feeling for value differences. He experiences all things as being of an equally dull and grey hue, as not worth getting excited about, particularly where the will is concerned. The decisive moment here—and one that is denied to the *blasé*—is not the devaluation of things as such, but indifference to their specific qualities from which the whole liveliness of feeling and volition originates. Whoever has become possessed by the fact that the same amount of money can procure all the possibilities that life has to offer must also become *blasé.*"[21]

d.   c.

22 Simmel,
    Sociology of George Simmel,
    344.

23 Ibid.

24 Ibid.

25 Theodor Adorno,
    " Functionalism Today,"
    trans. Jane O. Newman and John H. Smith,
    Oppositions 17 (Summer 1979):
    31.

26 Immanuel Kant,
    Critique of Judgement,
    trans. Werner Pluhar.
    (Indianapolis: Hackett,
    1987), 77. (§16).

thus transforms mere possession into the sensuous and emphatic perceivability of the individual himself. . . . And this is so, not *although* adornment is something "superfluous," but precisely *because* it is. [22]

For Simmel, adornment, because it is superfluous, expands far beyond the narrow compass of the necessary and the individual: "the superfluous 'flows over,' that is, it flows to points which are far removed from its origin but to which it still remains tied: around the precinct of mere necessity, it lays a vaster precinct which, in principle, is limitless. According to its very idea, the superfluous contains no measure."[23] Thus, against Mies's "less" Simmel proposes "more," a more linked intimately to the processes of the money economy:

> In the *adorned* body, we possess *more*; if we have the adorned body at our disposal, we are masters over more and nobler things. . . . It is, therefore, deeply significant that bodily adornment becomes private property above all: it expands the ego and enlarges the sphere around us which is filled with our personality and which consists in the pleasure and the attention of our environment. This environment looks with much less attention at the unadorned individual, and passes by without including him. [24]

But this criterion, as Theodor Adorno points out as early as 1965, can easily be reversed, given the right historical conditions, if, for example, the unornamented, as in the twenties, becomes a way of drawing attention. Indeed, Adorno is critical of casting the problem of ornament in these terms at all, terms that pose the "good" return of ornament against its "bad" exclusion. Such was the way of much postmodernism, which fell into the same trap as Loos himself, when, following Kant, he rigorously distinguishes between the ornamental or purpose-free (*zweckfrei*) and the functional or purposeful (*zweckebunden*) [e.]. For, as Adorno points out, the very definition of what is or is not purposeful changes with time; it is a historically determined category. This is illustrated easily by the perception that often "what was functional yesterday can . . . become the opposite tomorrow."[25] Indeed criticism of ornament is often no more than the rejection of something that once had functional and symbolic significance and has lost it. Ornament and nonornament are so historically interconnected, Adorno argues, that their separation becomes a block to thinking about design. Even if we rigorously try to avoid, as many functionalist modernists did, any trace of expression in design, when this work is viewed historically it inevitably is seen as the very expression of its age. Thus Adorno (in 1965!), concludes against both modernism and its opposite:

> On the one hand, the purely purpose-oriented forms have been revealed as insufficient, monotonous, deficient, and narrow-mindedly practical. . . . On the other hand, the attempt to bring into the work the external element of imagination as a corrective, to help the matter out with this element which stems from outside it, is equally pointless; it

When we judge free beauty (according to mere form) then our judgement of taste is pure. Here we presuppose no concept of any purpose . . .; our imagination is playing, as it were, while it contemplates the shape, and such a concept would only restrict its freedom. But the beauty of a human being . . . or the beauty of a horse or of a building (such as a church, palace, armory, or summer-house) does not presuppose the concept of the purpose that determines what the thing is [meant] to be, and hence a concept of its perfection, and so it is merely adherent beauty. . . . Much that would be liked directly in intuition could be added to a building, if only the building were not [meant] to be a church. A figure could be embellished with all sorts of curlicues and light but regular lines, as the New Zealanders do with their tattoos, if only it were not the figure of a human being. [26]

e.

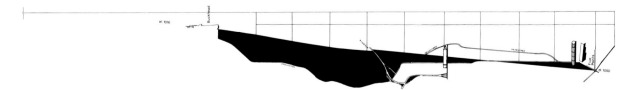

27 Adorno,
 "Functionalism Today,"
 35.

28 Ibid.,
 38.

29 Ibid.,
 39.

30 Ibid.,
 41.

serves only to mistakenly resurrect decoration, which has been justifiably criticized by modern architecture.[27]

The problem lies, Adorno argues, in the way of formulating the question in the first place: the posing of handicraft and imagination as two apparently exclusive terms. Even as handicraft, conceived as anti-art, too easily degenerates into an unimaginative or even antitechnological materialism, so imagination, conceived as the untrammeled expression of the individual, easily falls into the trap of personal, as opposed to public, willfulness: "Where only such expression is striven for," Adorno notes, "the result is not architecture but filmsets."[28] Both, when pursued as goals in and of themselves, forgetting that they exist also for others, become fetishes. The argument falls into a contradiction that pervades modernism and its critics:

> On the one hand, an imagined utopia, free from the binding purposes of the existing order, would become powerless, a detached ornament, since it must take its elements and structure from that very order. On the other, any attempt to ban the utopian factor, like a prohibition of images, immediately falls victim to the spell of the prevailing order.[29]

The division between the useful and the useless then fails to resolve, even though it explains, the contradictions of the object in modern society.

What Adorno is suggesting, of course, is not that these contradictions can ever be overcome, by some overarching and essential definition of usefulness and uselessness in art, the nonornamental and the ornamental, but precisely that such definitions will always be the response to specific historical conditions, which continually demand reflection and analysis. He suggests that the architect engage in what he calls "constant *aesthetic* reflection" and self-criticism to avoid the all-too-easy lapse into self-justifying hypotheses and the defense of fixed intellectual constructs [f.].

> Such an aesthetics would not presume to herald principles which establish the key to beauty or ugliness itself. . . . Beauty today can have no other measure except the depth to which the work resolves contradictions. A work must cut through the contradictions and overcome them, not by covering them up, but by pursuing them.[30]

Adorno's notion that the object of art is not a given, that "aesthetic thought must surpass art by thinking art," would, over twenty years later, suggest an excellent corrective for the expressionist formulas of postmodern or deconstructivist "constructs."

If we return in conclusion to the projects with which we began, taking them as the built signs of their respective architectural positions—Scogin Elam and Bray's Buckhead Library and Eisenman's Wexner Center—we can now see them as "thinking through" the apparent Kantian polarity of "ornament/nonornament" in different but related ways so as to dissolve or "overcome"

KIPNIS *Without, I won't call it sophistication, but, a simple cognizance of the systems, provisional or not, in which value judgments are operating, you don't really have judgment at all. We're all ready to bemoan comments like "Well I don't know anything about art but I know what I like." But we have to become more and more sensitive to how that logic permeates an architectural press, an architectural* reportage *and value judgments. In a sense, if we're constantly writing prolegomena, preparations for judgments, it's because judgment without such preparation is the most violent form of activity. It's not that I think anyone here has failed to take responsibility, we've just prepared the stage for taking responsibility. That lacking, we give stage to violence.*

f.

the apparent contradiction. Proscribing both functionalism and ornamentalism, they dress down their monumentality for a postmodern culture that signifies no longer by sharp distinctions between "high" and "low" but rather by a field of differences among endlessly reappropriated languages. Here codes are assimilated and stressed alternately to blend in or stand out of context. This said, of course, "dressing-down," with its double implications of cultural disguise and "telling off," is still a patently high-cultural and thereby powerfully monumental act.

Such an observation leads to a different interpretation of the contemporary "ornamental monument" than that provided by Vattimo through Heidegger. In place of a "weak" background, we still see a strong foreground dedicated to the most full expression of individual and contextual values. In place of a meditative state of "post-history"—that too often in the past has opened itself to a dangerous nostalgia—we find ourselves still immersed in the continuing struggle of historicity. At once the greatest open secret of patronage and the very condition of patron's architecture, ornament then, within the terms of the philosophy of money, becomes the site of a debate over the relative values of patronage and the public realm.

TALLAHASSEE OFFICE BUILDING

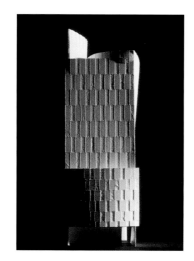

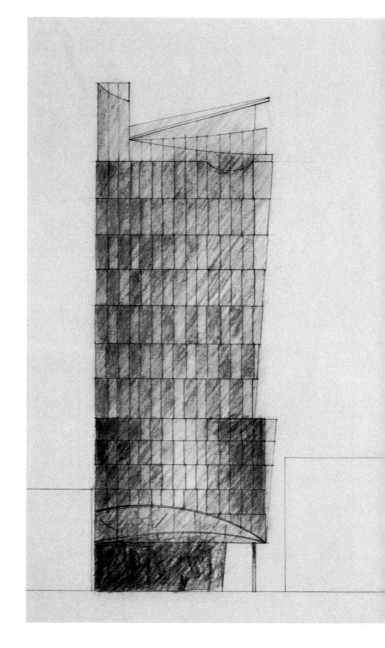

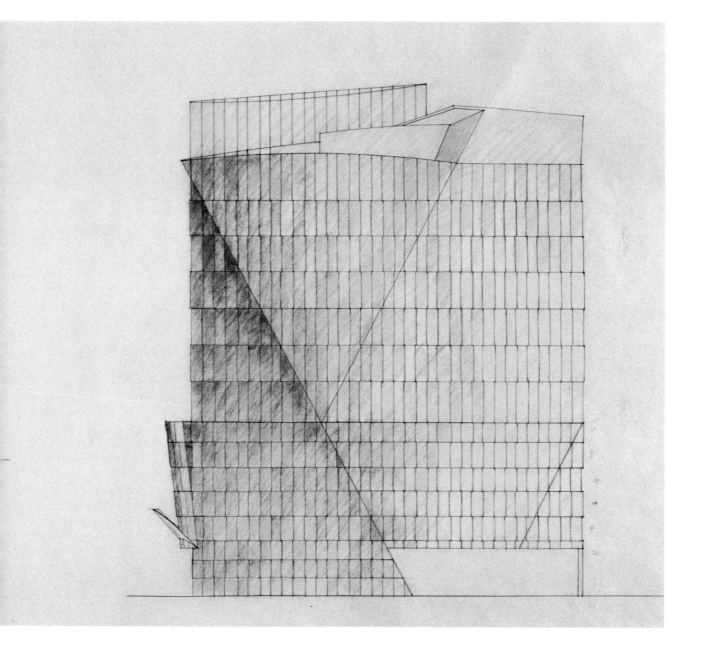

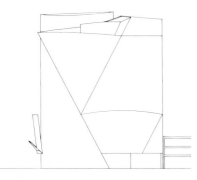

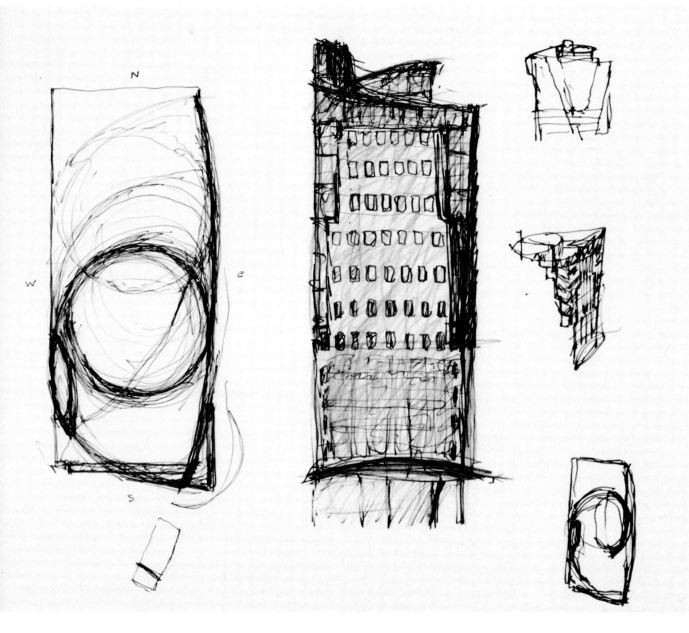
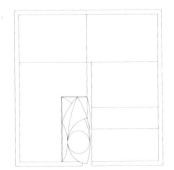

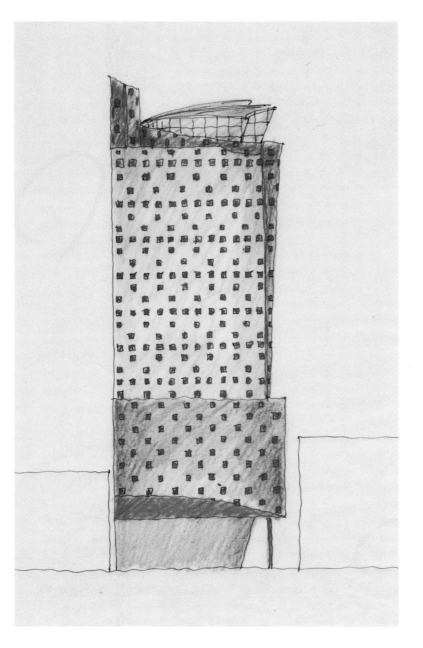
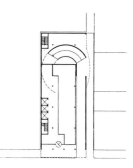
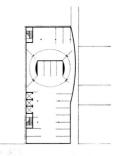
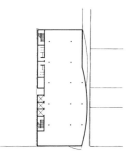

HIGH MUSEUM AT GEORGIA PACIFIC CENTER

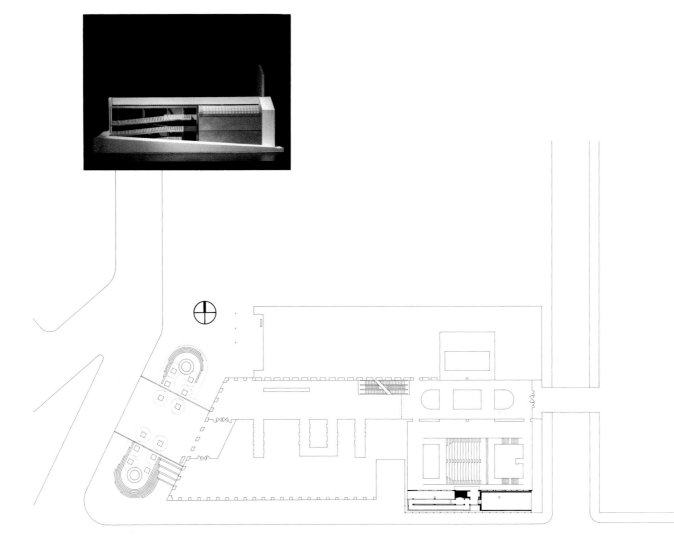

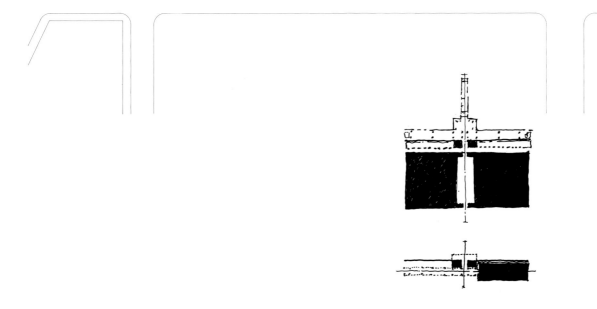

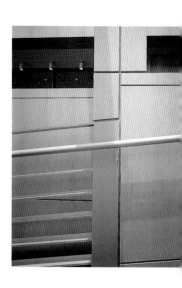

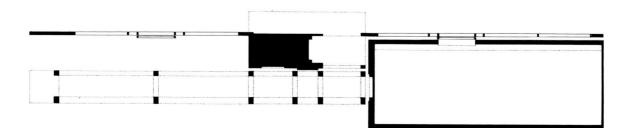

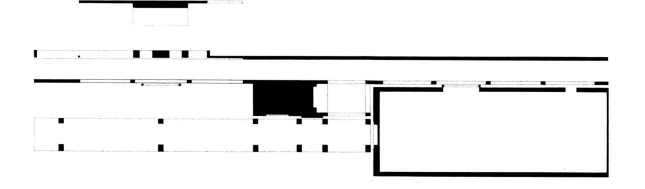

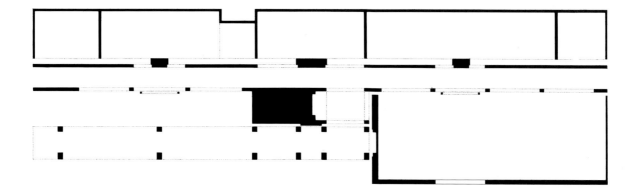

The Architecture of Difference: Engagement and Representation in the Work of Scogin Elam and Bray

Alan J. Plattus

1 Ferdinand de Saussure, *Course in General Linguistics* (New York: MacGraw-Hill, 1959), 120.

Difference is a meaning-making machine. Indeed, we now recognize that it is embedded in the very structure and mechanism of language itself [a.]. As such, it has been a ubiquitous and unavoidable strategy of cultural production, even in that long era—premodern, if you will—when the primary goal of such production was the creation of resemblance, not difference. Already in the seventeenth century Claude Perrault recognizes that it is the difference of the classical orders, one from another, that produces meaning, not their imitation of an external, objective Nature. However, in that context, with the exception of certain special historical and spatial precincts in which it is allowed to flourish in relative safety, difference may be an important linguistic or rhetorical device but is rarely an end in itself. Difference comes into its own from the late eighteenth century on, with the redefinition of the project of culture as "critical" rather than merely constructive, celebratory, affirmative, or legitimating.

In architecture, as in other disciplines, that critical project begins as anticipatory diagnosis rather than as a full frontal assault on the conventional institutional and theoretical structures of architecture. The monsters inhabiting the mannerist margins of Renaissance culture, the glimpses of Enlightenment rationality gone mad in Piranesi's *Carceri* and Goya's black paintings, the incipient collapse of architectural language and typology in Lequeu's fantasies and Piranesi's *Campo Marzio*, and the increasingly radical heterogeneity of the modern industrial city as depicted by countless novelists, artists, and social critics all provide a preview of difference as the disruption, rather than the positive mechanism, of the continuously articulated and proportioned body of traditional architectural theory and space.

Indeed, if traditional architectural theory, in both its Aristotelian and Cartesian versions, advances its arguments and, by analogy, its buildings by a logical process leading from first principles to applications, from part to whole, from body to building to city to cosmos, then critical theory starts not with a *tabula rasa* but with a critique of, and differentiation from, the status quo, including its theoretical rationalizations and mystifications. Even if its goal is, ultimately, that of a clean start on a clean slate, its very structure is implicated in and even determined from the outset by its starting point in an attack on some version of an existing condition, crisis, pathology, or ideology. Its theoretical weapons are forged for that attack and are rarely subsequently abandoned if and when it turns from critique to construction. Difference is, therefore, not merely another tool for critical theory and practice, it is the very warp and woof of its discourse, as well as being, in many cases, the principal goal of its practice.

Furthermore, what we might call the metalinguistic function of difference has been inextricably bound up, from at least the nineteenth century on, with its political function. The meanings created by linguistic difference or, conversely, obscured by fictive resemblance, are recognized

In language there are only differences. Even more important: a difference generally implies positive terms between which the difference is set up; but in language there are only differences *without positive terms*.[1]

a.

2 de Saussure,
Course in General Linguistics,
115.

3 Jennifer Bloomer,
"In the Museyroom,"
Assemblage 5
(February 1988):
60.

188

now as never having been neutral, natural, or objective. Increasingly the ostensibly neutral binary structures of formalist theory, structural linguistics, and semiotics are seen to describe contested terrain. Unmasked and revealed as repressive ideology and not simply descriptive semantics, difference is made available as a banner for movements of cultural, ethnic, sexual, and racial identity and even liberation [b.]. Thus difference becomes not only a mechanism of meaning but the engine of the avant-garde. To make culture in the modern age is not only to make meanings but to clear out the space for that project through an explicit or implied critique of the arbitrary and repressive boundaries of the existing cultural field. Small wonder, then, that difference has become not only a commonplace of contemporary critical discourse but, in a curious reversal that often begins with the "critique of representation," itself a stock subject for representation in contemporary cultural production. One can now discuss the iconography of difference in modern architecture and architectural theory. Here "difference" can, for a moment (perhaps its last), recover, through the deployment of the same old rhetorical strategies inherited from centuries of mainstream Western culture, some of the energy and force lost in the course of constant reiteration, analysis, and critical dissection in countless academic journals and Ph.D. dissertations. It becomes, in that context, an unimpeachable hallmark of "critical artistic practice," a sign of itself and of the persistence of the avant-garde ambition that has been its main sponsor for over a century.

In architecture one possible starting point for a "critical" history of difference is the "theoretical" writings of Piranesi as they emerge in the early 1760s. Not only is Piranesi driven to write theory in the largely polemical context of a response to neoclassical claims for the priority and superiority of Greek architecture, that theoretical enterprise becomes the occasion for a positive account of his own radical strategies of graphic and architectural production, hitherto presented under the curiously modest banner of mimetic archaeology. If, in retrospect, Piranesi's monstrous eclecticism has earned a secure place in the genealogy of the avant-garde [c.] [d.], the status of Augustus Welby Pugin's *Contrasts* of 1839 is more ambiguous [e.]. On the one hand, Pugin's sponsorship of a historically, linguistically, and ecclesiastically purified Gothic revival is a response to the Pandora's box of stylistic and cultural difference pried open by eighteenth-century historiography and archaeology and the romantic eclecticism that followed in its wake. Pugin is also, of course, concerned to condemn what has been seen, from his time on, as the privileged site of social, political, and visual heterogeneity—or, in Pugin's view, anarchy and degradation—namely, the industrial city. Nevertheless, his linkage of art and society in the differential diagnosis of cultural pathologies is a crucial plank of the avant-garde platform, however reactionary his purposes. Even more important, however, is his invention of a powerful graphic correlative for Thomas Carlyle's critical juxtaposition of "Past and Present." The wickedly

Even outside language all values are apparently governed by the same paradoxical principle. They are always composed:

(1) of a *dissimilar* thing that can be *exchanged* for the thing of which the value is to be determined; and

(2) of *similar* things that can be *compared* with the thing of which the value is to be determined. Both factors are necessary for the existence of a value. 2

John Soane kept Piranesi in the closet. . . . The Piranesi scratchings are contained within the *poché* of the house that Soane built. 3

b.   e.   c.   d.

4 Manfredo Tafuri,
*Architecture and Utopia:
Design and Capitalist Development*,
trans. Barbara La Penta
(Cambridge: MIT Press, 1976),
ix.

5 Jacques Derrida,
Of Grammatology,
trans. Gayatri Spivak
(Baltimore: Johns Hopkins
University Press, 1974),
44.

incisive plates of *Contrasts* are its most lasting legacy and stand, somewhat ironically, near the beginning of a tradition of visual and spatial polemics in which "this" representation is deployed to kill "that" pathological condition.

Certainly the avant-gardists of the twenties like Le Corbusier were masters of the rhetorical polemics of difference and beneficiaries of the sharper graphic tools of their time, although in setting the figure of the Voisin plan against the ground of the old city of Paris Corbusier precisely reverses Pugin's argument [f.]. He also produces an image of difference in which the effect is far more compositionally dependent, even parasitic, upon the articulation of the joint between the old city and the brave new world of modernism. The aesthetics of the joint, first at level of the city and later internalized in the project, have been central to the modernist discourse of difference, whereas Pugin's romantic medieval utopia is, by definition, more self-contained. Both, however, use a rhetorical strategy of difference to cancel the real, and therefore disturbing, heterogeneity of the industrial city and stylistic eclecticism. Indeed, Pugin would have recognized and approved the need to cross out the mere styles purveyed by the academy, if not the series of linguistic reversals proposed as a replacement. Once forged, however, these polemical instruments and strategies of difference can, like Frankenstein's monster, turn against their inventor, as the postmodern cancellation in turn of its antagonist and accompanying reversal of charges clearly demonstrates [g.] [h.].

These X's do not, of course, stand for the provisional erasure of Derridean *différance*, although taken together in the collapsed space of post-history rather than in historical sequence they may amount to the same thing [i.]. Indeed, that is precisely the problem to which we have already alluded [j.]. The representational history of difference seems to chart the endless deferral and displacement of the actual project of difference, as each performance in the accelerating inward spiral of the avant-garde mainly sets the stage for the next polemical cancellation or reversal. Whether that next gesture is initially in the name of a "truly radical" difference or a return to the cultural unity of resemblance seems to matter little, since the one turns quickly into the other—avant-garde difference into monolithic stylistic homogeneity and arrière-garde revival into rampant eclecticism. It appears that the more inventive the critical project becomes in its attack, frontal or parodic, on its chosen antagonist, the more it exhausts itself at the level of representation, providing, increasingly, mainly a caricature of its own linguistic means—in this case "difference."

It is hardly surprising, given the dynamics of difference in contemporary avant-garde practice, that the critical project of first-generation postmodernism quickly degenerated and provoked, in turn, its own characteristic reactions.

The "endgame" of the avant-garde has by now been described countless times, although reports of its demise always seem to be premature. The most powerful critique of the architectural avant-garde in relation to the problems to which I allude is still Manfredo Tafuri's *Architecture and Utopia*, and his eloquent pessimism with respect to the possibility of a critical architecture, as well as his notorious statement of preference for "silence" in the face of that condition, which could well serve as epigraph and envoi to this essay.

One is led almost automatically to the discovery of what may well be the "drama" of architecture today: that is, to see architecture obliged to return to *pure architec-ture*, to form without utopia; in the best cases, to sublime uselessness. To the deceptive attempts to give architecture an ideological dress, I shall always prefer the sincerity of those who have the courage to speak of that silent and outdated "purity;" even if this, too, still harbors an ideological inspiration, pathetic in anachronism. 4

The
Inside
X
the
Outside 5

j.   i.   f.   g.   h.

Contextualism, for example, initially a response to the sterility of orthodox modernist urbanism and a defense of the cultural and spatial heterogeneity of the traditional city, soon became a recognizable style in which certain plan gestures and graphic techniques came to stand for a concern with, and responsiveness to, "context." As style, contextualism seems complicit with, rather than resistant to, the hegemony of the very forces against which it formulated its agenda, producing not the radical difference of critique but the consumable difference of the commodity. Ironically, one version of contextual postmodernism which never eschewed the problem of the superficial image for the presumptive substance of "urban space" and the phenomenology of place and symbol may have sustained its critical energy the longest. Eventually, however, it too fell victim to the reification and stylization of its own critical representational strategies.

The jury is still out on the latest wave of postmodern revisionism, and even Charles Jencks has yet to get a handle on its stylistic characterization. Clearly it seems determined to succeed precisely where its predecessors have failed and so once again initiates a version of the critical project mainly as a critique of its chosen antagonists and the wide-eyed rediscovery of neglected alternative paths in the history of the recent past. In this respect, however, it may be possible to discern some preliminary tendencies and themes, such as the affiliation, more or less explicit, with post-structuralist theory, an interest in the early (pre-CIAM) modernist avant-gardes, a fascination with the heterotopian modernism of Alvar Aalto and Carlo Scarpa, or, alternatively, a commitment to the tectonic fundamentalism of Louis Kahn. However divergent or incompatible these tendencies may seem—and that in itself seems symptomatic—they share an (un)common ground in the thematics of difference. It is the central issue and irritant that leads to and from that alarming range of reference. In this situation most recent neo-avant-garde architects have latched on, very tightly, to one specific issue or direction, in a curious and suspicious parallel to recent single-issue politics. However, one testament to the remarkable virtuosity of the work of Scogin Elam and Bray is that it seems to embrace all of these directions, if not simultaneously then at least within a very short period of time. Thus, not only is difference an issue and a strategy in their work, one can perhaps use that work to construct a veritable case study of its function in contemporary architectural discourse [k.].

Let us take, for example, the firm's Atlanta Chamber of Commerce Corporate Headquarters of 1987 and Herman Miller Showroom of the next year. A conventional critic might ask, in mock horror, if these two projects could really be by the same architects, while a post-structuralist critic might discern a displacement of authorial intention, since the firm has published them together, along with the Kahnian High Museum at Georgia-Pacific Center and the Aaltoid Clayton County Library. In fact, they are all linked, however tenuously, by a commitment to that characteristic

KIPNIS *In any of these papers the fertility of the graft between commentary as frame for work, or work as frame for commentary, is abundant. The real question is, "Is that going to be true for any architect's work?" Because if it is, then nothing is said. If it's true that the architecture is a road map for the criticism and we could have gotten any body of work at all and grafted the commentary today with all of its diversities and similarities onto it, then we are really faced with a crisis, an aporia. If any architecture, period, can participate in the themes in general, there would be a bankruptcy.*

k.

theme of difference. The Chamber of Commerce Building encodes urban and programmatic difference in a conspicuously subtle and self-consciously dumb way. It is a brilliantly understated little building, and while it is very knowing (knowing quite a lot about the unholy alliance of Venturi, Aalto, Corbusier, and rationalism), it is hardly fashionable. The Herman Miller Showroom is, however, like its client (so far from the bourgeois boosterism of the Atlanta Chamber of Commerce), all about fashion. No ordinary brick here but new wave materials and treatments in support of what must be one of the first actually built "deconstructivist" interiors, the founders of that movement having rather less established local client bases. The tightly contained, highly wrought and beautifully detailed dynamism of the showroom wears its difference on its sleeve. Indeed, it stands as an emblem of the disjunctive, fragmentary, and ephemeral aesthetics of difference ostensibly derived from the experience of the contemporary city, even as the project seals itself off from any real contact with that city [l.].

Here indeed is another point of contrast between the two projects. While the compositionally explosive dialectics of the showroom lie buried in a suburban office park—originating, as the architects put it, only at the front door—in the simulated urban realm of one of Atlanta's precocious edge cities, the Chamber building is situated on a very "real" urban site, where the disjunctions of the modern city hardly need to be represented, since they are unavoidable. The dominant

strategy of the Chamber building in relation to its interstitial site is apparently a rational—and rationalist—deployment of the stabilizing figure of a largely symmetrical and hierarchically centered building. It is only on second and even third glance that one recognizes the lopsided asymmetrical inflection and the bilateral tension that threatens to cleave building and site in two, as much as (re)unify it. The Chamber building is all the more provocative for introducing difference at a

secondary gestural level, whereas the showroom is all differentiated gesture. In this respect, the showroom is like the more aggressively anthropomorphic postmodernism of the seventies, which leaves very little to the empathetic imagination. The showroom overacts, brilliantly, while the Chamber building shrugs, laconically.

One can make too much of geography and the marginal suburban location of the showroom compared to the urban site of the Chamber building. It is, however, intriguing that Scogin Elam and Bray's two projects in downtown Atlanta are also their most conventional (not to say conventionalized). On the other hand, the deconstructive aesthetic seems to take root and flourish in the suburban fringe. This is both ironic and predictable: ironic insofar as most critical accounts of, and claims for, such an approach relate it to contemporary urban instability and fragmentation as well as to social and ethnic differences and marginal discourses largely trapped in the urban core, when not displaced by gentrification; predictable in that the loose context of suburbia both allows and necessitates the largely self-referential sculptural display of difference that characterizes the firm's more recent work. Projects like the Chmar House and the entry building for the Herman Miller Headquarters in Michigan seem to explode their full charge of difference where it will do the least good or, for that matter, the least harm. The beautiful pedestrian bridge at what is oxymoronically called "Concourse" seems to stand in the midst of a quintessential edge-city

landscape (known, even more oxymoronically, as Perimeter Center) as a symbol of the loss of any real public realm, whether based on difference or consensus. It speaks, as the architects have suggested, of the desire to connect two points, but there is nothing here to connect, and so it is just as much a *ponte rotta* as the bridges in Piranesi's *Carceri*.

It is, after all, precisely the possibility of that public realm that is at stake, and not only in Atlanta, where it must do battle with the incipient loss

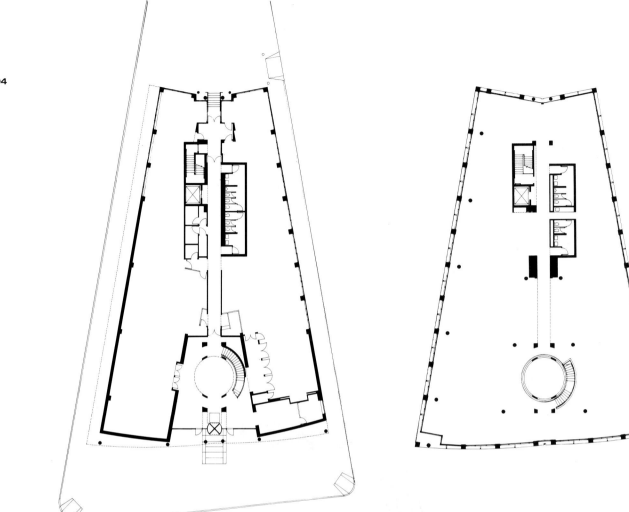

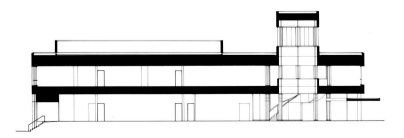

6 See Mary McLeod,
"Architecture and Politics in the Reagan Era:
From Postmodernism to Deconstructivism,"
Assemblage 8 (February 1989),
23–59.

of the downtown street to the skyways connecting the interior landscape of convention center, Portmaniac atrium hotels, and shopping malls. The desperately real differences of the contemporary American city have no place, even as representation, in that pseudo-public realm, in the spaces proposed by revivals of monumental urbanism in the City Beautiful tradition, or traditional neighborhoods in the Garden City tradition. Here, at least, the critique leveled by the neo-avant-garde has some force, and the fresh public imagery proposed by projects like the Clayton Library has considerable poignancy—very much in the American tradition, from the County Courthouse to Robert Venturi and Denise Scott Brown, of making the ordinary extraordinary. But when that critique becomes a self-referential meditation on the aesthetics of difference (with fashionable allusions to the impossibility or irrele-

vance of a public realm in the age of microchips), at the expense of those for whom the possibility of a space of difference is of more than academic interest, we are dangerously close to that condition of postmodern aestheticization diagnosed by Mary McLeod—not just of architecture but more ominously, as Walter Benjamin predicted, of politics as well.[6] It is not yet clear whether Scogin Elam and Bray's trajectory from the habitable and homely heterogeneity of the Clayton Library—one of the very best public buildings of the 1980s—to the fashionably decorated shed of the Buckhead Library, with its transformation of public port-cocher into deconstructivist ornament, points to a general move in the same direction. If, however, the route from Clayton to Buckhead and from the Chamber of Commerce in downtown Atlanta to the showroom in Edge City does describe a trend, then it appears to be away from actual engagement with the city and the ordinary landscape as a space of difference and toward a largely representational manipulation of difference as style.

7 See Diane Ghirardo,
"Two Institutions for the Arts,"
Out of Site: A Social Criticism of Architecture
(Seattle: Bay Press, 1991),
114–119.

8 Steven Connor,
*Postmodernist Culture: An Introduction to
Theories of the Contemporary*
(London: Basil Blackwell, 1990),
79.

9 See Mike Davis,
*City of Quartz: Excavating the
Future in Los Angeles*
(London: Verso, 1990).

Just as the stylization of context signals the deflation of the critical project of contextual post-modernism, such a stylization of difference signals the absorption of the neo-avant-garde critique into the general problematic of postmodernism. This is by no means a new discovery. Critics such as Diane Ghirardo have noted the tendency, for example, of Peter Eisenman's built work to deflate the critical pretensions of his theoretical pronouncements, where radical disjunction is manifest as pleasurable representation.[7] Other critics have connected this tendency in architecture to postmodern discourse in general:

> [I]t is common to argue that postmodernist architecture rejects univalent style in favor of an exploration of multiple styles, the incompatibility of which gives this architecture its ironic energy. But this exploitation of stylistic difference depends crucially upon a theoretical self-consciousness "in" the building or assumed to be in its viewer which is sufficiently intense to allow awareness of the forms of incompatibility. But, as well as giving awareness of the forms of difference, such self-consciousness may also act to give unity and coherence to these forms of difference. As with Foucault's "heterotopia," the announcement or theoretical recognition of heterogeneity always to some degree flattens or precludes the possibility of such heterogeneity.[8]

How much more so, one might add, when heterogeneity becomes not merely the object of theoretical recognition but the subject of architectural representation—no longer in the familiar tradition from mannerism to Piranesi to Lequeu, or from Furness to Aalto to Venturi, of contamination of codes, but as difference per se. It is the very abstraction by means of which architectural difference is now encoded as clashing grids, vectors, and objectified traces, however sensuous their material manifestation, that threatens to drain any remaining critical and political capacity from that hard-pressed theme.

Perhaps, after all, difference belongs in the streets whence it came. That is where one might actually "make a difference" rather than making of difference a more or less sophisticated spectacle [m.]. The modern city is already precisely such a spectacle, far more radical than any representation we could make of it, and while the function of such representational activity may be to call our attention to the political and social agenda of difference, it just as often provides a comfortably framed and contained escape from it, as in those microcosmic enclaves of urban difference as formal play constructed by Frank Gehry amid the genuinely radical heterogeneity of Los Angeles and elsewhere.[9] If Manfredo Tafuri condemned the nostalgic attachment of the avant-garde to the "utopia of form," we now have the "heterotopia of form" as a further strategy for warding off urban anguish. But a less formally ambitious architectural acknowledgment of urban difference, such as Scogin Elam and Bray suggest with a project that will never make the coffee-table histories of postmodernism, the Chamber building, would return our gaze—and not just our gaze—

PLATTUS *It's relatively self-indulgent when we talk about individual buildings and talk about "ideas" and "texts" and things like that in the midst of a lot of the really tough problems that exist in this city and other cities. So one does tend to get a little bit apologetic. There's a lot of apology built into contemporary criticism. We all qualify endlessly.*

KIPNIS *What I have heard today is no apology. When you read criticism in the newspaper it is operating on certain grounds of self-evidence. Every time I read, say, Paul Goldberger, it's not that I think that he's wrong in his observations. My contention is that he's correct in his observations yet grounding his value judgments on uncritical terms. I believe theory and criticism's job is to constantly undermine the systems of self-evidence so as to keep judgment on its toes.*

m.

10 Richard Sennett,
The Conscience of the Eye:
The Design and Social Life of Cities
(New York: Alfred A. Knopf, 1990),
225–6.

to the streets, rather than trapping it within endlessly fascinating and irrelevant formal sophistications. Here Richard Sennett's call for an *ethics*, rather than an aesthetics, of deconstruction touches a much anaesthesized nerve:

> Difference, discontinuity, and disorientation are also the principles of a certain kind of architecture which calls itself deconstructive. . . . What the deconstructive impulse particularly rejects is the idea that an ethical sense of self-limits arises from the experience of discontinuity or the creation of disorienting things. Discontinuity and disorientation figure instead as opening the gates to a more *enraged* relation to the world. . . . Perhaps this vision has become, oddly, too comfortable by now, the artist or critic knowing how to make those gestures which make the signs of rage and disaffection, like a well-rehearsed ballet of subversive gestures. Perhaps indeed a more truly uncomfortable idea is that difference, discontinuity and disorientation ought to be ethical forces which connect people to one another. Viewed this way, the ethics of difference, the moral value of exposure to others, the creative act of disorientation, recall the experience of sympathy, as it was championed in the Enlightenment.[10]

Even if we can no longer imagine a return to the Enlightenment public realm, we can at least construct what Lefebvre has called a "space of difference." In that space difference is recognized and engaged rather than merely represented. Representation does, after all, shift our meaning-making machine of difference into the neutral gear of *différance*, where not only meaning, but action, is endlessly deferred.

HERMAN MILLER, ATLANTA

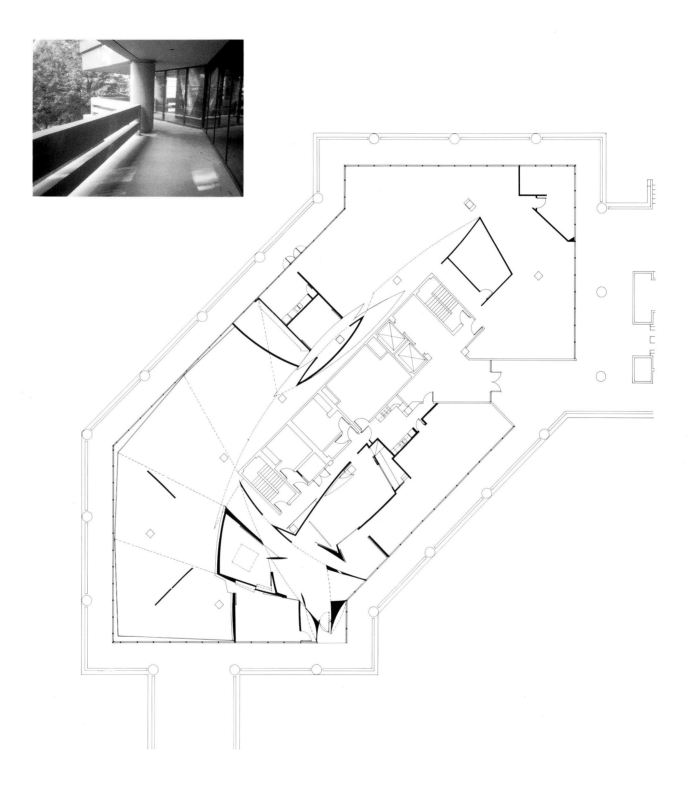

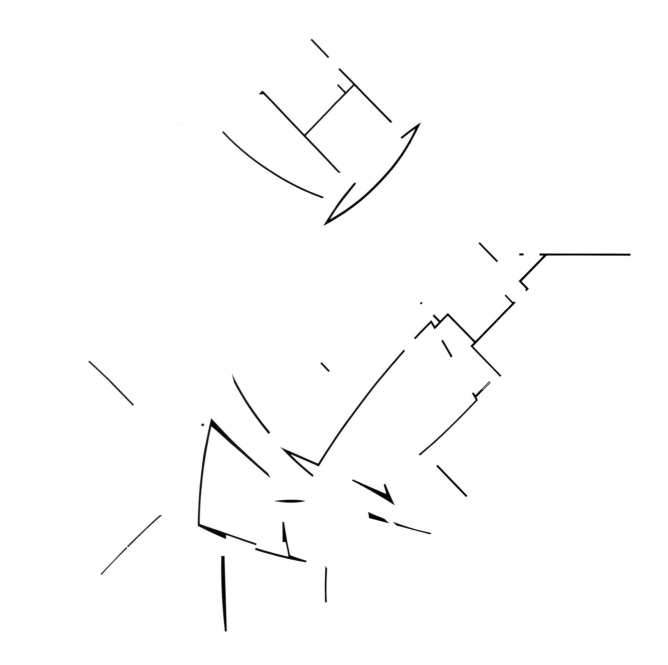

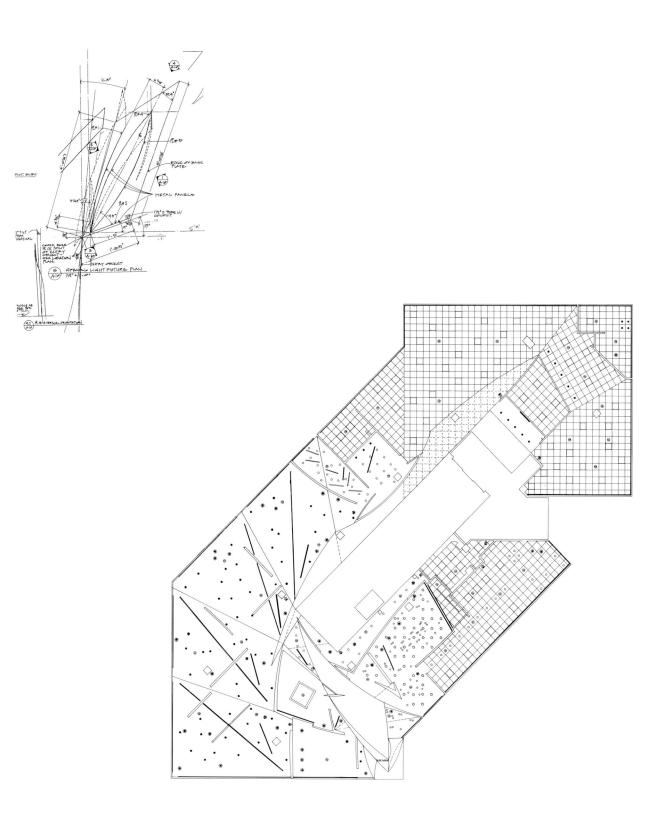

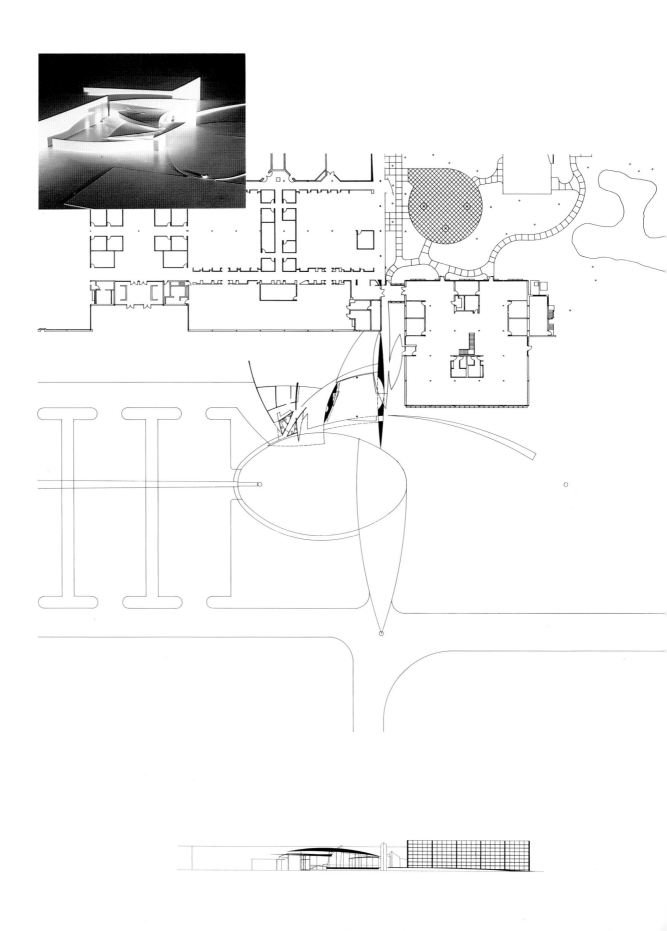

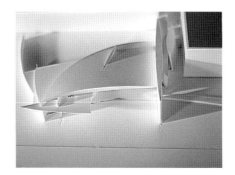

Biographies

MACK SCOGIN

Mack Scogin is a principal of Scogin Elam and Bray Architects, Inc., Atlanta, and Chairman of the Department of Architecture at Harvard University's Graduate School of Design, where he also holds the Kajima Chair. Scogin received a Bachelor of Architecture degree from the Georgia Institute of Technology in 1967.

Scogin is a corporate member of the American Institute of Architects, past Chairman of the Steering Committee of the AIA National Committee on Design, and a founding member and member of the Board of Sponsors of the Architecture Society of Atlanta. He was previously President and Chief Operating Officer, Director of Design, with Heery and Heery Architects and Engineers, Inc. in Atlanta.

MERRILL ELAM

Merrill Elam is a principal of Scogin Elam and Bray. She received a Bachelor of Architecture degree from the Georgia Institute of Technology in 1971 and a Master of Business Administration degree from Georgia State University in 1983.

Elam is a corporate member of the American Institute of Architects, founding member and past president of the Architecture Society of Atlanta, member and past president of the Georgia State Board of Architects, and member of the Board of Directors of *Art Papers* and of the 20th Century Art Society of the High Museum of Art. She has lectured and taught at Mississippi State University, Auburn University, Harvard University, the Southern California Institute of Architecture, Clemson University, and Ohio State University. She has served as the Harry S. Shure Professor at the University of Virginia and the William Wayne Caudill Visiting Lecturer at Rice University.

LLOYD BRAY

Lloyd Bray is a principal of Scogin Elam and Bray. He received a Bachelor of Architecture degree from Tulane University, and was previously a project architect and associate at Heery and Heery.

Bray has served as Vice Chairman of the Board of Sponsors of the Architecture Society of Atlanta and also on the Board of the Associates of the Atlanta College of Art.

MARK LINDER

JEFFREY KIPNIS

Mark Linder is Assistant Professor of
Architecture at the Georgia Institute
of Technology and is currently serving
as Adjunct Assistant Professor at the
University of Illinois, Chicago. He has
also taught design, criticism, and theory
at Rice University and Yale University.
His essays include "Architectural
Theory is no Discipline" in *Strategies in
Architectural Thinking* (Chicago: Chicago
Institute of Architecture and Urbanism,
1992) and "*MEMOI*_{res} Eye I" in
Architecture in the Eye of the Hurricane
(Clemson Journal of Architecture,
1992). His articles have also appeared in
the *Journal of Architectural Education*,
Arquitectura, and *Architecture and
Urbanism*. His built work includes
several residential projects in New York
and Connecticut.

Jeffrey Kipnis is Assistant Professor of Theory and Design at the School of
Architecture at Ohio State University. He has been a visiting professor
at Harvard's Graduate School of Design, the Cooper Union, and Columbia
University, and has lectured throughout the United States and Europe. He has
published numerous articles including "Architecture Unbound: Consequences
of the Recent Work of Peter Eisenman" in *Fin d'Ou T Hou S* (London:
Architectural Association, 1985); "Drawing a Conclusion" in *Perspecta 22*; and
"Though to My Knowledge" in *Restructuring Architectural Theory* (Evanston:
Northwestern University Press, 1988); and has contributed to *Assemblage*,
Architecture + Urbanism, and *Progressive Architecture*. He has published *In the Manor
of Nietzsche: Aphorisms in and around Architecture* (New York: Calluna Farms
Press, 1990), and has contributed to *Choral Works*, on the Jacques Derrida/Peter
Eisenman collaboration at Parc de la Villette (in Paris), forthcoming from
Rizzoli.

Jennifer Wicke is Associate Professor of Comparative Literature at New York University and has held positions at Yale University and Columbia University. She attended St. John's College in Sante Fe, the University of Chicago, and Columbia University. Her books include *Advertising Fictions: Literature, Advertisement, and Social Reading* (Columbia University Press, 1988) on the uses of literature in late-nineteenth-century newspaper advertising and the forthcoming *Consuming Subjects: Gender, Modernity, and the Work of Consumption*. Her essays have appeared in *ELH*, *Representations*, *Yale Journal of Criticism*, *Critical Quarterly*, and *Transition*. In 1988 she was awarded a Mellon Fellowship from the Whitney Humanities Center at Yale.

Ann Bergren is Associate Professor of Classics at UCLA and Adjunct Professor at the Southern California Institute of Architecture. She has been published in journals of classical studies, including *Arethusa*, *Classical World*, and *Helios*. She has also studied design at the Southern California Institute of Architecture and worked in the office of Eric Owen Moss. Her articles on contemporary architecture have appeared in the *Yale Journal of Architecture and Feminism*, *Harvard Architectural Review*, *Princeton Architectural Journal*, and *Assemblage*. She has been a fellow of the Chicago Institute for Architecture and Urbanism and the Center for Hellenic Studies in Washington, D.C.

ANTHONY VIDLER

ALAN PLATTUS

Anthony Vidler is William R. Kenan, Jr., Professor of Architecture at Princeton, where he has taught history, theory, and design since 1965. He is currently chairman of the Doctoral Program in Architecture and has been Director of the European Cultural Studies program. He served as a Fellow of the Institute for Architecture and Urban Studies and was an editor of the journal *Oppositions*. His books include *The Writing of the Walls* (New York: Princeton Architectural Press, 1987), *Claude-Nicolas Ledoux* (Cambridge: MIT Press, 1990), and *The Architecture of the Uncanny* (Cambridge: MIT Press, 1992). He is currently working on a book on space in modern architecture and urbanism.

Alan Plattus is Associate Dean and Adjunct Associate Professor of Architectural Design and Theory at the Yale School of Architecture. He is also an urban design consultant and has served as Chairman of the Flushing Meadows Corona Park Task Force. In collaboration with Diana Balmori, he designed an urban greenway along the route of the abandoned Farmington Canal in New Haven, a project that was awarded a Connecticut AIA Public Space Award. He is the editor of the new edition of *The American Vitruvius: An Architect's Handbook of Civic Art* (Princeton Architectural Press, 1989) and is currently compiling a companion volume, *The New American Vitruvius*, on contemporary urban design.

Bibliography

216

1992

Linder, Mark. DUMBFOUNDED ARCHITECTURE . . . ENOUGH UNSAID. *Architecture and Urbanism*, June 1992, 64–71.

Stein, Karen D. HANDS-ON ARCHITECTURE. *Architectural Record*, May 1992, 86–93.

SCOGIN ELAM AND BRAY. *Architecture and Urbanism*, June 1992, 72–118.

SCOGIN ELAM AND BRAY, ARCHITECTS. *GA Document 32* (1992): 92–117.

1991

Allen, Stanley. REThinking the PRESENT. *Arquitectura 289* (October 1991): 42–56.

Forgey, Benjamin. SPELLBOUND AT THE LIBRARY. *Washington Post*, March 23, 1991, D1.

Gandee, C.K. ATLANTA ALOFT. *House and Garden*, January 1991, 82–89.

HOUSE CHMAR. *GA Houses 30* (1991): 32–45.

Rash, Horst. RESPECTING NATURE: HIER BLIEB DIE NATUR UNANGETASTET. *Hauser*, April 1991, 16–23, 90–91.

Stein, Karen D. TREE HOUSE. *Architectural Record*, April 1991, 76–85.

1990

ATLANTA CHAMBER OF COMMERCE CORPORATE HEADQUARTERS. *Office Age*, (August 1990): 30–37.

Ivy, Robert, Jr. DOWN AT THE CROSSROADS: REGIONAL DESIGN FINDS A STRONG NEW VOICE. *Southern Accents*, May 1990, 52–60.

Barrière, Philippe. U.S.A. D'EST EN OUEST. *L'Architecture d'Aujourd'hui*, October 1990, 134–44.

DUE PONTI IN UNA PIAZZA PIENA D'ACQUA: PONTE AD ATLANTA. *L'Architettura*, May 1990, 363–65.

Fox, Catherine. ATLANTA ARCHITECTURE FIRM CHARTS INNOVATIVE COURSE. *Atlanta Constitution*, May 10, 1990, G1, G5.

___. EMBRACING THE VERNACULAR: ATLANTA'S SCOGIN ELAM AND BRAY ELEVATE THE ORDINARY TO ART. *Southern Accents*, September 1990, 48–54.

LA TO NY. *Quaderns*, November 1990, 56–61.

LO SPAZIO CHE RIMALZA: SHOWROOM AD ATLANTA. *L'Architettura*, March 1990, 204–5.

Murphy, Jim. FOCAL POINT. *Progressive Architecture*, December 1990, 66–73.

___. MEANING FROM CHAOS. *Progressive Architecture*, December 1990, 60–65.

PONTE PEDONALE AD ATLANTA. *L'Industria della Costruzioni*, January 1990, 38–41.

Welsh, John. BIG MACK. *Building Design*, October 25, 1990, 24–25.

___. BUILDING ON THE BIG IDEA. *Building Design*, November 23, 1990, 10.

1989

Scogin Elam and Bray Architects. *Architecture and Urbanism*, November 1989, 39–134.

Andersen, Kurt. A Compelling New Modernism. *Time*, January 2, 1989, 92–93.

Attrative Bibliotecarie. *L'Architettura*, July/August 1989, 540–41.

Freeman, Allen. Practical, Unpretentious, Open, and Family Oriented. *Architecture*, May 1989, 158–61.

Scogin Elam and Bray. *9H* 8 (1989): 94–103.

Stein, Karen D. Spatial Craft. *Architectural Record*, June 1989, 98–105.

1988

Brenner, Douglas. Defying Gravity. *Architectural Record*, September 1988, 114–17.

___. Art on the Rise. *Architectural Record*, Mid–September 1988, 60–63.

Cullum, J. W. On Southern Identities and Difference: Marginal Notes for Mack Scogin and Merrill Elam. *Assemblage* 7 (October 1988): 87–91.

Design Award: WQXI Radio Station. *Progressive Architecture*, January 1988, 99–101.

Downey, Claire. In Progress: Turner Village, Candler School of Theology, Emory University. *Progressive Architecture*, March 1988, 52.

Fox, Catherine. Daring Design. *Atlanta Journal*, May 29, 1988, E1.

Freeman, Allen. Museum Grafted Onto a Tower. *Architecture*, May 1988, 184–85.

Murphy, Jim. K-Mart for Information. *Progressive Architecture*, November 1988, 82–89.

Projects for Two Libraries. *Assemblage* 7 (October 1988): 57–86.

1987

Downey, Claire. In Progress: Buckhead Branch Library; Clayton County Library System Headquarters and Main Branch. *Progressive Architecture*, August 1987, 40.

Cullum, J.W. Mack Scogin: The Making of an Intuitive Architecture. *Art Papers*, July/August 1987, 20–25.

218

1986

Brenner, Douglas. THE FRAMER'S ART: THE HIGH MUSEUM AT GEORGIA–PACIFIC CENTER. *Architectural Record*, November 1986, 124–31.

Elam, Merrill, ed. *Art Papers: Architecture in the Land of the Secret Formula*, July/August 1986.

IN PROGRESS: WQXI RADIO STATION. *Progressive Architecture*, April 1986, 41.

Scogin, Mack. BROTHER DICK AND THE JESUS PEOPLE. *Art Papers*, July/August 1986. Filmstrip.

1985

Elam, Merrill, and Susan Desko. A PARKING LOT STUDY. *Art Papers*, July/August 1985, 26–27.

Scogin, Mack. A BRIDGE FOR THE LANDMARKS GROUP AT CONCOURSE, ATLANTA, GEORGIA. *Art Papers*, July/August 1985, 22–23.

1983

Elam, Merrill. HOMAGE TO T.J. In *The American Dream*, edited by Claire Downey, 63. Atlanta: Georgia Institute of Technology, 1983.

Stevenson, William. TOWER TO SOUTHERN MEMORIES: 1983 ARTS FESTIVAL OF ATLANTA. *Art Papers*, May/June 1983, 2.

Scogin, Mack. ERNEST ANGLEY LIVES THE AMERICAN DREAM. In *The American Dream*, edited by Claire Downey, 69–73. Atlanta: Georgia Institute of Technology, 1983.

Design Awards

CHMAR HOUSE
AIA National
Honor Award, 1992
> Georgia Association AIA Citation, 1990

CLAYTON COUNTY LIBRARY
National AIA/ALA Award for
> Excellence 1991
>> AIA National Honor Award, 1989
> South Atlantic Region Conference AIA Honor Award, 1989

WQXI RADIO
> Progressive Architecture Award, 1988

BUCKHEAD LIBRARY
National AIA/ALA Award
> for Excellence 1991
> Georgia Association AIA Honor Award, 1990
Urban Design Commission Award
> of Excellence, 1990

HIGH MUSEUM AT GEORGIA PACIFIC CENTER
> AIA National Honor Award, 1988
> South Atlantic Region Conference AIA Honor Award, 1987
> Urban Design Commission Award of Excellence, 1987
> Gallery and Museum Association of Georgia, Outstanding Museum Award, 1986
> Georgia Business Council for the Arts Award, 1986

SILVER MEDAL, ATLANTA CHAPTER AMERICAN INSTITUTE OF ARCHITECTS, 1989
Firm award, five years of design excellence

Project Credits

APPLING/MCGREGOR HOUSE

Mack Scogin with Merrill Elam and Lloyd Bray; Isabelle Millet, John Lauer, and Jeff Atwood

NEW VISIONS GALLERY

Merrill Elam and Mack Scogin with Lloyd Bray; Criss Mills, Susan Desko, and Sean McLendon

CHMAR HOUSE

Mack Scogin with Merrill Elam and Lloyd Bray; Susan Desko

TURNER VILLAGE, CANDLER SCHOOL OF THEOLOGY

Mack Scogin, Merrill Elam, and Lloyd Bray; Jeff Atwood, Susan Desko, John Lauer, Leslee Hare, Frank Venning, Criss Mills, Carlos Tardio, Denise Dumais, Monica Solana, Roy Farley, Jane Seville, Christine Gorby, and Sean McLendon

BRIDGE AT CONCOURSE

Mack Scogin with Merrill Elam; Lloyd Bray and Dick Spangler

CLAYTON COUNTY LIBRARY

Merrill Elam, with Mack Scogin and Lloyd Bray; Tom Crosby, Rick Sellers, Dick Spangler, Isabelle Millet, and David Murphree

WQXI RADIO

Mack Scogin and Merrill Elam; Lloyd Bray, Susan Desko, W. Ennis Parker, Rick Sellers, Jo Anna Estes, Tom Crosby, Dick Spangler, John Lauer, Gilbert Rampy, and Isabelle Millet

BUCKHEAD LIBRARY

Mack Scogin and Merrill Elam; Lloyd Bray, Susan Desko, Jeff Atwood, John Lauer, Ellen Hooker, Patricia Kerlin, Ron Mitchell, Isabelle Millet, Criss Mills, Carlos Tardio, Roy Farley, and Sean McLendon

TALLAHASSEE OFFICE BUILDING

Mack Scogin with Merrill Elam and Lloyd Bray; Frank Venning and Jane Seville

HIGH MUSEUM AT GEORGIA PACIFIC CENTER

Mack Scogin; Merrill Elam, Lloyd Bray, Dick Spangler, Gilbert Rampy, Isabelle Millet, George Johnston, John Lauer, and W. Ennis Parker

ATLANTA CHAMBER OF COMMERCE

Mack Scogin with Merrill Elam and Lloyd Bray; Dick Spangler and W. Ennis Parker

HERMAN MILLER, ATLANTA

Mack Scogin, Merrill Elam, and Lloyd Bray; Frank Venning, Susan Desko, Monica Solana, Carlos Tardio, Jeff Atwood, and Criss Mills; Doug Zimmerman, Rick Van Gelderen, Dyan Van Fossen, and John Scholten of Herman Miller, Inc.

HERMAN MILLER, MICHIGAN

Mack Scogin with Merrill Elam and Lloyd Bray; Frank Venning, Jane Seville, and Jeff Atwood

Photo Credits

NEW VISIONS GALLERY

All photographs by Timothy Hursley

CHMAR HOUSE

All photographs by Timothy Hursley except pp. 54 and 62 (lower) by Mark Linder and p. 64 (upper) by Merrill Elam

TURNER VILLAGE, CANDLER SCHOOL OF THEOLOGY

All photographs by Timothy Hursley except p. 86 (lower) by Lloyd Bray

BRIDGE AT CONCOURSE

All photographs by Timothy Hursley except pp. 113 and 118 (upper) by Ann Bergren and p. 115 (upper) by Merrill Elam

CLAYTON COUNTY LIBRARY

All photographs by Timothy Hursley except pp. 122 and 128 by Brian Gassel, pp. 123 (middle) and 125 (lower) by Mark Linder, and p. 133 (upper) by Ann Bergren

BUCKHEAD LIBRARY

All photographs by Timothy Hursley except pp. 158, 159, 168, 171 and 172 by Brian Gassel and pp. 163 and 166 (upper, lower right) by Lloyd Bray

HIGH MUSEUM AT GEORGIA PACIFIC CENTER

All photographs by Timothy Hursley

ATLANTA CHAMBER OF COMMERCE

All photographs by Timothy Hursley

HERMAN MILLER, ATLANTA

All photographs by Timothy Hursley

Ann Bergren: pp. 120 (snapshot right), 136 (snapshot)
Lloyd Bray: pp.16, 23, 24 (upper), 75 (upper), 107 (upper), 120, 142, 143, 149, 174 (left), 177 (lower three), 178, 191, 210, 211
Merrill Elam: pp. 102 (upper), 179 (snapshot)
Mark Linder: pp. 20 (context n., p.), 86 (upper)
Alan McGee: pp. 46, 47, 48
Snapshots by Mack Scogin and Merrill Elam: pp. 11, 18 (j.), 24, 33, 45, 61, 64, 75, 76, 79, 88, 99, 110, 116, 145, 146, 147, 157, 164, 171, 184, 205
Courtesy of dub: p. 22   Courtesy of John Portman Associates: p. 70
Courtesy of John Weber Gallery: pp. 17, 18
All other photographs and drawings courtesy of Scogin Elam and Bray

Post Script

LINDER *Does criticism have a real effect upon the practice of architecture? Are we vain to imagine that criticism actively participates in the making of architecture?*

VIDLER *It may be that there is no simple, linear relationship between what a critic says about a building or an event and what an architect does, but certainly if the architect listens and pays attention to other aspects of experience in the world, it cannot leave that architecture unchanged. The irritation with critics like Paul Goldberger is just as much a part of the architect's life as the critic's.*

KIPNIS *The system, the mechanism, for the way the information starts to insinuate itself on practice is actually the most interesting problem of all. If Tony will forgive me for telling a private anecdote, I heard him say, "You know, I show a few slides of Ledoux at Princeton and the next thing you know, it's Michael Graves, and then I do a paper on the uncanny and all of the students are doing haunted houses."*

VIDLER *That was at Georgia Tech! Seriously, if you're experienced you realize that there is not a cause and effect relationship between those events. There is something culturally such that at a certain moment both Michael Graves and myself are interested in Ledoux for our own reasons.*

KIPNIS *It's not a question of cause and effect, nor a question of separate but equal. There is a kind of transmography (the only way I can talk about it) in the way an idea infects and influences practice and the way that practice is inflected under the name of the idea.*

LINDER *But the confounding question is, why is some of the most critically acclaimed architecture emerging in places where people seem to feel unconstrained by critical discourse?*

KIPNIS *They are colluding consciously or unconsciously. There is a collusion between critical discourse and practice.*

LINDER *In many cases the collusion is a strategy to get commissions and notoriety. On the other hand, most professionals are suspicious of investing a lot of political and theoretical sentiment in their practice. The point of being an architect is to win competitions and get more and more buildings built. I know I'm being polemical but I'm trying to represent what seems to me to be a prevalent view held by people who are are very successful and, in fact, producing work which attracts immense critical attention.*

THE WORK OF SCOGIN ELAM AND BRAY

CRITICAL ARCHITECTURE

ARCHITECTURAL CRITICISM

"Criticism occupies the no-man's-land between enthusiasm and doubt, between poetic sympathy and analysis. Its purpose is not, except in unique cases, either to eulogize or condemn."
Alan Colquhoun

ANN BERGREN
PROFESSOR OF CLASSICS, UCLA
Artimesia, Aristotle and the View from L.A.

JEFF KIPNIS
ASSISTANT PROFESSOR, SCHOOL OF ARCHITECTURE, OHIO STATE
Picking up the Pieces

ALAN PLATTUS
ASSOCIATE DEAN, YALE SCHOOL OF ARCHITECTURE
The Architecture of Difference

ANTHONY VIDLER
PROFESSOR, PRINCETON SCHOOL OF ARCHITECTURE
Critical Theory – Theoretical Practice

JENNIFER WICKE
ASSOCIATE PROFESSOR OF ENGLISH AND COMPARATIVE LITERATURE, YALE
Building a Practice: Regionalism/Internationalism/Globalism

Made Possible Through: Fulton County Arts Commission
Architectural Society of Atlanta; Georgia Tech Architecture Program
ASA Implementing Architecture Fund;   Georgia Tech Ph.D. Program

SATURDAY, MAY 12 9:00 – 6:00
HILL AUDITORIUM HIGH MUSEUM OF ART

PLATTUS *When I go see buildings by another architect, often ones that I would never make myself, I still realize that we both had read the same book at about the same time, we both were seeing a certain other architecture through the eyes of that text. I'm not talking about a sense of deep community. I am simply talking about a pervasive culture within which the interpretations of buildings— buildings themselves and experiences of buildings—interpenetrate in unpredictable ways. I think Tony was alluding to that as well. I happened to have been a student, then teaching at Princeton when some of these funny kinds of things took place.*

VIDLER *There's also a great deal of dissimulation. When I go out and see Frank Gehry, for example, he's saying, "Yeah, I'm just sitting around in my little patch here doing this and this and this." But he is one of the most sophisticated readers of surrealism and dada.*

LINDER *Yet that's other art work, not criticism in the sense we've been talking about it today. The architects I am thinking of do not consider themselves to be linked together by a set of books, but because they like the same artists or saw the same buildings. I wonder what it is they learn from the work critics do. Many architects would say that critics are in the game of perpetuating themselves. Do critics presume the value of criticism? Is a critical forum, or criticism in general, valuable to architects?*

SCOGIN *Let me see if I can give you a real simple answer. We've never had a group of six people sitting around talking about our work. Now that's of value to us. I'd like to go to Korea and Merrill's dying to go to South America. Every new experience is of great value. Our work is not "critically acclaimed." We're virtually unknown in the world of architecture. So this is a new experience from which we will learn something.*

BRAY *I would answer your question in this fashion. To me, architects read the culture and their work manifests what their reading of the culture is.*

We find a lot of interest in roadside attractions and this is another roadside attraction.